EROTIC SHOWERS

SHOWERS of EROTIC SHORT STORIES & POETRY

SUMMER BRADSHAU
Your Poetic Mistress!

ISBN-13:978-0991115952
ISBN-10: 0991115953

DEDICATION

This book is dedicated to those who will support the effort of helping humanity through respect and love along with a great sense of humor and the desire to shower with us.   I write the story, you create your vision!

EROTIC SHOWERS OF SHORTS

POETRY IN MOTION

"I write the story, YOU create the vision!"

Your *Poetic* Mistress

EROTIC SHORTS

Birth Of Erotic

The Erotic Shower Birthday One

(Team Sagittarius Nov)

Limo picked us up at 6pm... We had dinner on the delta with heaters on the dock... oh so hot... allowed us women to dress as beautiful as we wanted to on this chilly November night.

Dinner with candles and flowers and so... the men were well dressed and smelled rather nice if I may say so. The women made you want to lick them anywhere your eyes viewed and the smell of sweet yet strong perfume.

Laughter filled the air as did hands full of drinks. I think we need to eat (laughing out loud making our way to the buffet).

There was prime rib, filet Minot, salmon, stuffed mushrooms, rice pilaf, asparagus and the best tasting mash potatoes you will ever melt in your mouth... the butter...ooohhh.

The bread was freshly baked, and the salad seemed to contain the savor flavor of heaven and lettuce lol but if you close your eyes ... here ... taste some (I'm reaching the fork into your mouth, how nice).

Drinks were strawberry margaritas, sweet Carmel green apple martinis, Jack Daniel and of course her famous Crystal Champagne for the birthday girl toast!

The food was specially catered by her favorite chef flown in for the occasion, courtesy of him. He just loves serving up heaven for Summer B... she won't stop talking about it all year to everyone who will hear. That's his secret, he knows she will spread the word, a win win for everyone lol.

There was also a special request for Rainbow Sherbet Martinis by one of the ladies... naughty by nature.

We had personal rainbow sherbet pops and as we licked we dipped and sucked... oh what pleasure on a Popsicle stick (licking my sweet and sticky lips).
It cannot get any better than this... (But I know it will, just chill)

We laughed, enjoyed shade from the trees and then the desert came... (Hold on to me)

Two tables were rolled out of the kitchen each with dimmed lights that reflected 45 candles. Under the candles were a fruit and cake display…. one, her favorite strawberry shortcake and the other…. well… let's just say it's chocolate! -

The strawberry short cake display was that of a beautiful creation… a woman neatly placed on her back fully exposed as the strawberry shortcake was created on her … nipples and … other holes lol.

The strawberries were dipped in chocolate and the chocolate seemed to ooze in places I just wanna lick, but people are looking so let's move onto the chocolate… now that's the shit.

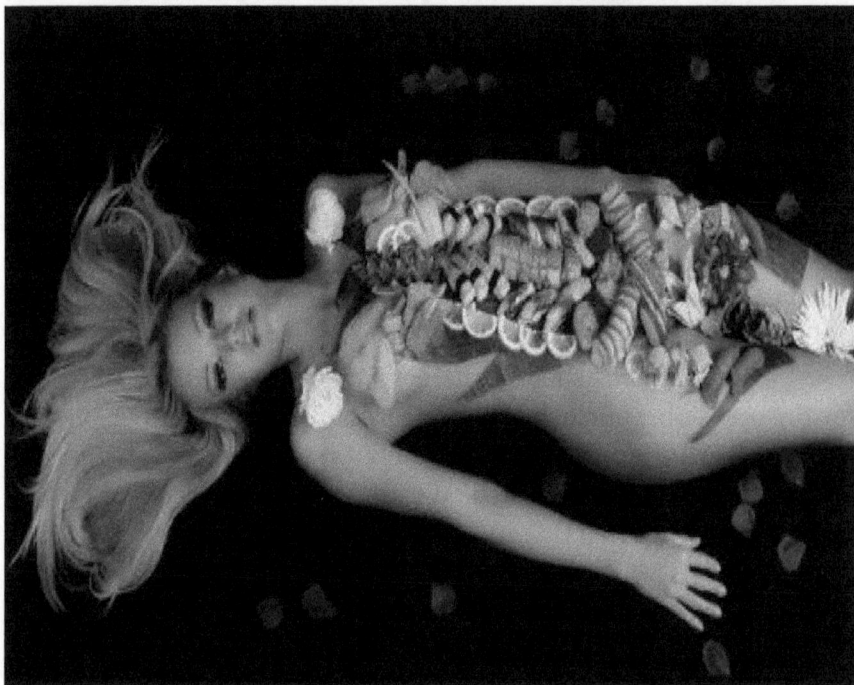

The chocolate display was that of a man…. HE WAS LARGE AND BALD AND HELLA FINE! His body was sculpted into a heavenly display of muscle and sweat, and he was hers for the day!
(It's part of her services… forbidden fruit displays)

Hip Hip Hooray! It's my fucking birthday!
On this cake there were chocolate everything, there were even nuts and lots of whip cream. Where in the hell do we begin?

EROTIC SHOWERS

On the count of three.... 1   2   3
HAPPY BIRTH   DAY   TO   YOU! HAPPY   BIRTH DAY TO   YOU

And many morrrrrreeeeee!
It took five whole minutes to make a wish and fifteen minutes to blow out all those damn candles... can somebody fan the smoke detector up in here lol.

Summer is laughing, and her glass is in the air as there is cake.... right there in her hair. Oh, how good that cake taste... licking melted chocolate and strawberry delight makes me want to get a to-go container... oh how clever.

Summer moves over to the chocolate surprise... oh nice. First, she tries the chocolate chips that are melting right on his nipples... no toothpick needed; she's coming in with just the grin. Over there are chocolate wafers dipped in ice cream at his groin, now that's devine, I want it.
She picks it up and dips with her lips licking and the girl is getting restless.... what is all this.

Ice cream is cold and makes the girl hot... how nice. Next stop is the banana topped with hot fudge and nuts. This is literally his penis, shut the fuck up!
She takes the banana into her mouth, coming back for small bites at a time, licking the chocolate that is surrounding the area, now that was clever, and the cream that's injected, are you sure that's not... (I'm just saying). Her mouth is full and is making her wet. Oooh we, this birthday shit is on hit!

The girl at this point is about to explode so... I WANT MY CAKE AND EAT IT TOO! She screams as she jumps onto the table with no underwear on!

Everyone is laughing and staring and screaming out loud as she eats her way into...chocolate land!

5

And in walks the man! Her man.... with a bottle of Crystal in his hand, his look on his face is like what the fuck is this but the smile is a smirk as she stops and takes her hand and puts her finger in her mouth like, fuck I'm caught and everyone is quiet except the music is still loud and the banana is in the girl ... what do we do... (Everyone sshhh and be still, maybe he won't know were here lmao)

HE HOLDS THE BOTTLE OF CRYSTAL IN THE AIR AND SAYS... "HAPPY BIRTHDAY BEAUTIFUL... don't hurt em baby"!

Everyone starts clapping and screaming cause they were scared for a minute and the fun ... it continued!

He walked over to where Summer B was injecting the banana and began to bite her ass that was so seductively in the air, she had hot fudge right there... really come here (nibbling).

That chocolate cake was her only date and the strawberry delight; he had to have a bite. Summer ventured over to where he was having desert and began to join him. No forks needed here... Mmmm taste like ... was that your tongue?

After the desert and lots of drinks... it's time to jump into the limo and get to the real fun!

Summer B ... and he takes a private limo the rest of the way. What? ... It's time to play!

Her legs are silky sweet and her toes you may want to eat... but when you get to the flavor of the girl... let's just say you will definitely say never, have you ever.... no other words needed! (Silent)

Her lip gloss taste of forbidden fruit the kind that only comes once in a lifetime. The kind that captivates your soul into submission.

Her skin glistened with 24 carat gold body shimmer that made her look edible with each move that she made. It came from France.

Her breast was smothered in the smell of ecstasy for two... Chanel (she doesn't disclose the rest lol).

Her earrings are diamond and hang like a tear... a tear of joy she says, a gift from him.

Her diamond ring sits petite and sends a ray of light throughout the limo with each move her beautiful finger makes. You can even from time to time see it shine right in her eyes... can you see?

She uncrosses her legs as she sips her drink. His lips are on her neck and the girl is getting weak.

It's time to change the music, something we can slow our roll to... we have a little ride before us and we want to savor the moment. Oh, do we want to savor the moment... (Head tilted back, and the legs open slight)

He takes his tongue to her neck and down to her breast as her lips, she licks, sticky from the drink and sticky from the thought of what is on its way down to happy land. I mean...

His tongue finds her navel as he twirls it some more and the way to the girl... no need for a map, just follow the rainbow! Whoa is that a pot of gold?

Her legs slightly open as does her lips, she wants to taste a piece of this... shit!

The window fogs and the heat is on... what in the world is the name of that song?

Here we go again, the message is in the music.... as the music is playing a beat that only she can hear but with each note, he can feel through her inner being. Sweet!

Of course, we have Kem singing sweet music to her ears and a taste of what Adelle may have to say... well just because it's the birthday we don't sweep issues away lol... keep it moving... on to the chic in the back of the limo with her mouth on his ... watch your mouth!

It's her birthday... her wish was to have her cake and eat it too and you saw the cake back there at the room, oooh.

Now back to you... close your eyes and imagine that you, the most beautiful woman or you the most handsome man are in the back of this limo with your one and only man or woman... now stick with the story and take the ride...

She (imagine it being you) is tasting chocolate that was brought over snuck in the bag for the trip, he opened it up and now it's in dip.

He (imagine it being you) pulls out the whip cream and nuts and applies to the fun. He gone mess around and spring one!

The two are a fit so perfect indeed, like the mold for each was complete... serious and freaky

The limo is hot, and the steam is getting thick, turn up the air condition, shit!

They stop at the bottom of the mountain on the way into Tahoe, where the fire is waiting in the private bungalow.

It's cold and there is snow and her nipples are showing but its ok because they got a snow bunny date. They stop to get pie and hot chocolate for the trip when they stumble upon the cutest little bunny on this side of the world that could ever exist.

He asks her name… check this… (With her winey little ass) "It's Princess"! WTF

And this bitch bastard takes that and laughs…I'm standing there looking like you must be tripping, flirting with this clear chic name princess. But ok… I'm down with the game.

"Hi baby, my name is Too Sweet", Summer says. And with that comes a giggle, where the fuck is we at kindergarten for gigabels?

He had the nerve to ask her how old she was… 32 she says!

(Me) Shut the fuck up…

She looks like she's 10 and with that comes the grin… this bitch bastard is all smiles now that he knows she's not jail bait lmao.

His penis is swelling I can see it from here. Oh, how cute now let me go over and rub it a bit.
Walking over to where he is she reaches for his pants and his smile gets wider as he continues talking with "Princess" who is going up the mountain to get some rest. Says she has been working hard for the family company and its time for a vacation. Five days in the mountains uninterrupted by nothing but danger.

It can't get any better than this…

The other limos pull in with the other partakers and the laughter is crazy, the stories are forever. They stopped here and did this and two of them made out in the woods, while the others found fancies and ways to connect there was even a stop to get laid in the snow while the others waiting in the limo. Wow, people do crazy things when it's cold outside.

Back to "Princess" ... He is talking and waving to the others who come over and say hello. She is smiling from ear to ear as their heads turn to look at Too Sweet and how she is taking this. She is smiling at them and greeting her friends, they are here to have fun so let the fun begin!

When they all jump in the limos the last one out is the Birthday Girl...
In the limo they fall in and the music begins... the driver asks if they wanted heat, no replied him for the heat will come from me!

I reach over as he hands me a drink and I pass it to Princess. She takes a sip and looks into my eyes. I take my drink... take a sip and look into her eyes.

He holds up his glass to toast the birthday girl. The two hold up theirs as they give praises and cheers and the music is so loud, but the fun just begun and what the fuck is the name of that song?

He is sitting in between the two women as his penis enlarges with each breath... I can feel his heartbeat. I can feel him sweat.

The girl is asking questions and wondering when the fun will begin. Sshhh...

Princess reaches over and pats him on the knee with her laugh. He pats back. She looks at him with her beautiful eyes and kisses his lips. He leans in with a stronger thrust down her throat, like there was no tomorrow.

The girl is on fire as she watches the two. The drink is almost gone, and she can't think of what to do.... so
He reaches over while kissing princess and puts his finger inside the girl... oh ok so that's what we do then.

EROTIC SHOWERS

TAKE THE RIDE....

Take the ride... in your own mind!

Arriving in Tahoe is a red door. Inside the red door is the ultimate party that you will ever want to be. And the guest list is sweet...

Birthday Party fit for a queen... Summer B

(As she sings "Happy Birthday To Me" walking in the door)
Her dress is red satin sweet silk divine, came off the Estate Lauder cover model.

Her walk is that of heaven on earth with each step that she takes remembering her grace as she kisses each face. She is happy as can be when she sees who is here ... let the fun begin!

The music gets cranked up and the people are dancing and drinking with the most fire I have seen in a while. The fireplace is large and is blazing so hot... I got a spot.

Sit with me as I take it all in...

Over walks the tray of fruit and a bottle of Crystal Champagne... six glasses and a grin... aw, my friends.

They walk over with a smile on their face, hugging and kissing and singing praise. But it's not about me it's about the blessing... the gift God gave me. But back to this party... wow! This is crazy!
I see Reece over there and look there is Vanessa and Deshaun. And Tracy just stepped out of the limo. Only the best and the elite are at this event. They even flew in Barnes, chief in government. He's a huge fan of "The Bradshau Hotel" with its private entry features and all, happy to show up at any event that's hosted by the misses.

WillyWill and Tito walk over to the bar and there they mix conversation with Herbert who will one day become their number one financer little do they know, I plan a hell of a show. Flock joins them. The guest list aren't just people to have fun, it's about what we can do for each other, each talent exposed.

The party had some of her favorite few; Pam and Sam were of course the first to arrive to make sure everything was complete. "The man" was a no show, not good for the two currently, but over there... bring your ass over here Johnny Blaze is in the house! It was his birthday a few days ago... Happy Birthday love!

This party is getting better and better unless you add in the fact that that dude over there is wearing leather... who the hell is that and what is in the front of his pants, oh my Gosh I can't help but to stare....Dick everywhere!

Now... someone had a gift on the table that was a large Gold box with Red bow. I couldn't help but to continue to stare as if it were different. My mind eventually ventured over and opened the top... SHUT THE FUCK UP!

The note read," I love You more than ever! Happy Birthday Beautiful one"!

It was 45 bottles of Crystal Champagne!!!!!!!!!!!!!! WTF, who gets gifts like this! This is the "excuse my French" shit! (You know I'm French right?)
The note also read, "45 bottles ...one for the next 45 years" ...

Here's to good friends, how sweet! (But you know how I drink right? lol)

Aw... the gift, it was from him, her man

There were politicians shooting the shit with everyday common folk, there were employees and family and anyone you would want to know. Bianca and Mia actually showed! The party was

12

off the hook from the moment it was created, and look at Slick over there, trying to play it nice. Her and AD are looking rather luscious!

The rest of the ladies, Mika and Twan are having the time of their lives, there are single men like crazy and that one... he has a wife. Here comes Trice and Mario and Shy in tow... whoa, This is so cool.

The food is to die for and the desert just the same but wait... IT'S TIME FOR CAKE!

And with that came a piece of a dream... at least to him it seemed. lol

A band was set up just on the stage and the music they started playing made her stop and stare...

I know that man that walked out on that stage is not KEM!!!!!!!!!!!!!!!!!!!!! Oh no....WTF is this? (She looks confused)

The chef rolled out the cake at about the same time this man starts singing and I CAN'T THINK OF WHAT THE NAME OF THAT DAMN SONG IS! ...

It's fucking Kem! (THE SINGER)

The girl is jumping up and down and I'm trying to keep my composure... it's my fucking birthday and the candles light up the moment.

Kem is singing "I found heaven in you" as my man is on one knee, with a ring! (My eyes do not believe this shit)

He has a ring and he is on his knee while Kem is singing he found heaven in me. The candles are glowing and asking for help, but my knees can't move in this fucking tight dress.... help!

He said, "The man I use to be is gone"!

It's right there inside your heart, as the music continues...

13

You're the love of a lifetime and I find my strength in you girl.... YES!

Yes, I say as I twirl my tight dress and my smile I change to a kiss!

The people have stopped breathing as the music played anticipating her reply as each minute went by...

Cheers erupt as he jumps off his knee and swoops her off her feet! Ooh wee Summer B what you gone do to me!

The lights flicker on and off and Kem says "congratulations to the couple, I turn the mic over to my friend" ... and who and behold steps out of the rim but El Debarge who starts singing...

"Such a lonely place without you" .... I cannot believe this! El Debarge and Kem... now you know I gotta be right back after this... I gotta hook my dude up for this shit! I'm just saying!

The people are having a great time, the drinks seem to never stop and the smile on Summer's face is that of.... an angel, if I may say so myself.

The waiter brings out the champagne for the toast; he takes the mic and proceeds to speak to his future wife...

Her girls, Kelly, Shenida, Nicole, Carmen, Tonya and more are standing close with smiles and tears as he takes her by the hand and sits her in the chair. His voice softly spoken as he looks her in the eyes... (I cry)

"You hide from love, so you are never hurt, and I can promise you that I will never hurt you on purpose. You keep your distance, so your expectations of others don't destroy your love for them, but I can promise you that I will remain forever by your side, for the rest of my life. (The tears are really falling in front of all these people who didn't even know I could cry)

You pretend to not care when you carry the care of the whole world inside your small but large heart. I promise that I will fill your heart with only love and protect it from the dangers of others. Your beauty is not what's on your outside, it's what's on your inside, and that's what I fell in love with. Your willingness to love, your desire to live. I promise that I will be your first, your last and your everything...for the rest of my life. Summer B I promise to love you unconditionally"!

(Kem starts singing; when you are standing here with me, I can see everything in me. You are the life that feeds the soul, girl you are everything divine. In your love I will learn my wings to fly, in your heart I will make my home, in your love I will come to you, here's to our love "I do", oh ... yeah!)

The cake that is tall and the candles still lit is rolled over at this moment as he says, "baby make a wish"!

And with that, she looks at him, closes her eyes and when she opened them, there as tears rolled down her face was a vision of.... her father.

She blinked twice and found the tissue ... her wish unspoken to anyone to hear except God.

The ladies run over to see the ring, bling bling lol and the men pull out the cigars. Her glow is that of the moon on a clear and crispy day.

The music gets cranking and the people get loud, the cake gets thrown here and fro... you know how they do.

When the night was all over and the two made their way to their private cabin, they held hands as they entered like two little kids.

He closed the door behind them, slapped Summer B on the ass and said to her as she walked down the hallway looking back shyly at him and then at her ring...

(He said) "Baby... you've just been Jinxed"!

15

EROTIC SHORTS ONE

Let's Meet Sam

Stepping out the elevator at the Bradshau hotel, you can smell her. It's a special perfume she orders, for it's no longer in America. Everyone wants to arrive in time to smell the brisk aroma that takes control of you as she strokes her way from the penthouse suite, everyone wants to get a whiff of Summer B ... Ms. B for you tho.

It's a rainy morning and Ms. B. is on her way to the office to put in a few hours. Her skirt is long, and her boots are tight and cute... ooh. Black, leather, pointy toe, with a cat walk heel, and rhinestone buckle. Did you say sexy ass hot chick? She is the shit... Her shirt is tight and with the rain and the cold you can see her nipples as her coat blows open.

Her hair is blowing in the crisp air and her lip gloss is catching her hair and making this look like a scene out of the movie. She is just the cutest thing trying to find her way into the building with all the wind blowing. When she arrives in the lobby, she lets out a deep breath and a smile and continues to her office in the corner looking over the Garden of Eden... she named it this because it's a garden of the beginning and the acknowledgement of sin.

You can go into the garden and have a smoke break on one section and you can lay back on lawn chairs and umbrellas in another section. One section has cots in the spring and summer with umbrella and a refreshment bar in the center. Ms. B likes to give everyone a chance to do what they need to do to ensure they are happy and focused.

It's time to get to work everyone...

Ms. B is a personal consultant and she takes on clients who would like someone to motivate them in their personal and or business life, someone to toot your horn so to speak. Give you positive energy and help you to become happy. Ms. B Upgrades those who desire more for themselves. So on to her client of the day.

Meet Sam. Sam Smith is a man who is well off. He owns his own architectural company. They are meeting at one o'clock on the dot to get started on his Upgrade. He is learning how to date again and after being married for almost 27 years and being recently divorced, Sam wants an Upgrade.

Sam wants to get laid. Sam wants to be all wrapped up into some coochie... Who knows how to date anymore after so many years? So, you call up Summer B and let her Upgrade you first ... It's that simple!

So back to the client, Sam is a great guy, low-cut, kind of shy but can be outgoing. Sam likes to have fun and cute if I may say so myself.

He is a little tight around that back side, his front makes your mouth water and makes you take a second look with a smile, and that chest can use a little lift but from where I'm standing... cute, I could do him (but I won't, it's my number one rule). Ok.... He alright... Let's get crackalackin!

Ms. B has to teach Sam how to date again. How to live a single life... So off they go. First stop, shopping. I don't know how men can go forever without going shopping for themselves. They don't even know what sizes they wear in anything... goodness.

So anyway, we are in the dressing room and out comes Sam with these jeans on that had his nuts asking me to come and rescue them. I was like whoa, no, those will not do. It's an experience and a half to get back into the world after being gone for so long but let's not give a pornographic view.

Out they come with a wardrobe fit for a king. New shoes, ties, shirts and anything needed for the Upgrade. Sam's step was a little bit higher when he stepped out of the boutique. Felt like a man for the first time in a long time. So, he is feeling hot and ready for the next move. Sam is looking rather smooth. Those balls tho ... moving on!

Summer's next move after shopping is to Upgrade the hair style. They go in and have a consultation with the main man, Leroy at Salon Manaz. Ever since Leroy, the best stylist in the bay, opened Salon Manaz, the Upgrades bring Ms. B about five hundred more per client just in presentation and referrals alone... The creations are from another planet.

They walk out of the salon looking like a million bucks and packing more testosterone than a gay Halloween party on the Castro. What? I mean...

Now this salon is of high status. There are no eight dollar cuts up in here so let's not get it twisted. Their clients in this beauty are paying a grip for what they get and it's well worth it.

So, they finish up with Leroy and Sam comes out ready to throw his thang .... Into somebody's thang.... And that's all that I'm saying. Right now, he can't even see straight.

He is feeling like "the man" ...Big Ups to Leroy and the folks at Salon Manaz, you're the man...kisses!

Sam has his own personal assistant, (MS. B) contracted for three months, who answers his call every morning as if he is the president of the United States. Who takes the task that falls from his lips and produces it without being asked? Who encourages you as you go through your day and sincerely blesses your every effort whether she likes it or not... I mean, who in the fuck gets a chic like that?

Even for women... those that have dared to hire Summer B. to Upgrade them have come back again and again. They were impressed with her professionalism and finesse. She is... the hot chick, with her Sassy little bitch.

What makes her hot? It's the way that she smiles.... You can tell she's sincere. I can hear her from here. Her smile says so many wonderful things. Like a rainbow of happiness all tied to a string. I mean... really, Ms. B is the shit. Ok... But she don't play... she will cut you! You do not want Ms. B to cut you...

So, the next move is here...

Sam has new clothes and a new wardrobe to boot. This fool is about to get into a new ride. He got cash and he got ass... he can get into a new Mercedes top of the class. I stop at the office and change, it's time to get sexy. Let's go see my friend Demetrious. He sells the top of the line every time.

I choose the little black dress with the spandex hips...We walk into the showroom with my little bitch Sassy. She is so cute, you must see her... anyway, I got on this hot ass dress that goes right to my knees but its tight and no sleeves if you can see what I mean.

It is black, and the neck comes down to my breast that is sitting up tight and you can't see anything else. My heels are sleek and sexy sues, my hair is up, and my scent is killing you. Introduced Sam to Demetrious and the two hit it off. Headed out to the specialty room.

Salesman leads the way, and everyone is happy. Summer B is skipping to a beat. Sam is thrilled, this is going to get ill.

The salesman looked weak like he was about to buckle when Ms. B passed in front of him to climb into the back door to see how comfortable the back seat was.

She asked him to sit in the back with her while Sam stood at the door looking in. The salesman felt weak and he looked excited too, his manhood was awake, and he was feeling good.

She smiled and laughed and told him a great story about how she and her friend used to meet in the backseat. The seat eventually became accustomed and so did the two.

he

So any vehicle that he buys must be comfortable enough for two... shit wouldn't you.

That shit is cool.

He is sweating while Sam is admiring the car... so far, it's five stars. So, Sam is smiling at the man and he tilted his head forward to let him know that it was ok to feel weak. She has the power to stop you where you stand and make your manhood come to command.

Makes you feel like a man, makes you feel like a woman. Her presence says everything, she needs not say a word, yet when she does, she makes you laugh and you get caught In Summer's World...

Sam wants the car with the sweat from their heat. As Summer stared him in his eyes as his heart stopped, waited, then skipped a beat. The salesman jumped out the car and ran inside and left her sitting there. She yelled, SOLD!

Over to Sam who laughed as he hard as he can. He could not believe what he was seeing and was laughing all the way to the bank. He got so much knocked off the sticker price; he took Ms. B over to the Louis Vuitton store and he bought a dog carrier for that bitch ass Sassy, so she can look hot too. Two hot chicks and an Upgrade with a dick... Now that's some shit!

We drive off the lot in the Mercedes fully loaded. Even threw in some cd's...sweet...

I got Sassy looking classy and I just got a raise. This man over here is feeling like king in his own parade. He cannot believe how good he feels, and it's only been a week.

He just started his Upgrade and he already has changed. How wonderful it feels. Small baby steps into large yet cautious leaps. Ms. B got yo back. That's Phat! And that's real!

Back to Sam... Now Sam wants to go out on the town and celebrate his Upgrade into Manhood. It's now officially one month in and Sam is making more money at work and saving money at home with Ms. B's Upgrade plan.

She scouts out your crap and helps you reevaluate things. Wow... what a wonderful feeling to have someone who sincerely cares.

Makes you forget the contract...

(I can feel his ass looking at me... ooh I can't' stand it. I have said a thousand times, don't like me and we can make millions. Everybody wanna fall in love, can't do business with anybody. Once you fall in love, you are chasing the pussy and not the money. Hell, the women start liking me too. Shoot. I got things to do. I don't have time to be trying to clean up your life after you hurt it. Stick with the contract. Eye's over there not over here... now can we please continue)

I am into my second month of Upgrade with Sam and he is quite the character man. He is handsome and cute and nice and tall but most of all, he wants to get laid. I met Pamela at the hot spot when I was out with Toni back in the day, she was this older lady with some bad ass shoes. I was like ooh, who you do? She laughed, and we became the best of friends.

I Upgraded her from a size 18 into a 10. Now, she wants a man. Well you know, a friend. Got a house and no bills and always seeking thrills. We had a blast doing her Upgrade. We have pictures and postcards; we went on trips, at her expense. She is the happiest woman who lives she says over and over again and it's been ten years.

She sends me postcards from all the wonderful places she's been. Now she is ready to settle in a man. She is cute, and her shape says a lot for her style. Her lips are thick and pouty and she's pretty when she smiles. I like the way her breast sits on her chest, they are the best.... Well, they are... geesh!

She and Ms. B have drinks by the fire. Pam has a house that is just bad. Fireplace makes you wanna get laid. I'm just saying, you know how I get down... So, the fire is going, and it starts getting hot... Pam tells me she is ready, so I make the call to Sam and invite him into the world of Pamela Fox. And for her age, this chic is hot.

In the Upgrade she received from Ms. B, Pamela was taught how to defend herself in bed... well, sordove. She learned how to have orgasms. She also learned how to suck a dick... well, really, she did, and did I mention she is the shit... and she don't use no spit. I told you this gone be some freakiness...

Who is a Guinea pig for that kind of shit? Young dick for a deposit on college tuition. It's hell of em...

You asked so... you know me; I'm just keeping it real. If you want an Upgrade by Summer B... you can find out for yourself how you can be all you can be up in here. She don't play.... What you need?

So, Ms. B gets Sam to shower, shit and shave... he is ready to misbehave! Sam is "the man" and he is rocking them jeans.

Shirt unbuttoned just a few because he knows what it do and ooh, he smells good too.

Pam is hell a cute and Ms. B is always fine, you mind? I didn't think so... So, we sitting in the lounge and the bar to my right, my shit is tight. Pam's house is old school like a fool, it's big and wide and bad as hell, who can I tell...well, this house is the shit.

Sam has arrived and is now drinking gin, oh my friend, where do I begin. So, he is sitting there, drinking and digging Pam for sure. She is blushing and carrying on. Looks like she is getting loose. She is starting to swing her skirt a little and she keeps pulling at her hair in the back like she's hot.

She can feel her heat rising, she can feel her thighs perspiring. She can feel that she wants some of Sam and from the look in her eyes she just told him just that. Matter of fact, Sam is leaning back, smiling, with his leg swinging open and his lip half ass. What type of shit is this? They are planning the whole thing in their minds, I can see it.

Sam walks over to Pam and puts his hands around her neck. She is sitting in the chair and he's standing from behind.

He bends over and smells her neck, I chuckle and shoot Pam a glance, she laughs. We some old as bitches in here giggling. I'm tickled...

Sam is rubbing her neck and asking her about her trips. She is smiling and enjoying the attention that he is giving. Sam has taken Ms. B romance class, and he knows how to treat her, how to spank that... ask her what's the secret, it's the way she demonstrates, crazy. "I get a standing O every time I lay down the wand".

Sam is the man when it comes to romance; he has learned and mastered the Summer B plan. He performs like a pro with a touch of a woman, gentle hands yet firm and securely alert. He is the mold of a man who Ms. B has created, not many around who can learn and withstand her commands.

See, Sam was willing because he knew he had no game, he had no clue what to do. So, Ms. B, the creator that she is, took Sam and turned him into the almost perfect man... The man every woman would want to be with... ooh wee! Ms. B!

Sam is about 6'2, perfect height, stands tall shoulders back. His legs are thick and hairy, butt is tight. His arms are muscular and his stomach the same, looks like he works out but that thickness and that shine, I wanna cry... ooh wee! You gotta see!

And his manhood that hears my name and knows when I'm in the room ...well wouldn't you? Shoot!

Sam has learned how to be the almost perfect man. He has learned how to be a little aggressive when needed as well as sincerity. He has learned how to say, no thank you as well as, will you be picking up the tab today? You see, women believe that the man is always supposed to pick up the tab. Not always the case.

If you are dating the same man, it is perfectly normal for the woman to share in picking up the tab when going out. Agree on what and who to be together. So, Sam has learned how to be a great boyfriend, friend and more.

He wants to explore, and Pam is sitting at his feet, by the fire on the floor staring into his eyes, listening to his every word as he is making her hotter than the flames that light the room. I am laughing to myself as the two acts like they have known each other for years.

Sam is very sexy as the light from the fireplace is glistening off his chest, I'm getting wet. Ms. Pam is laughing and feeling all sexy and Sam is enjoying the pleasures of the night. We are eating grapes and cheese and drinking Martinis and Gin and having a great time... I don't mind.

The music is hot and I'm dancing away, to the side of the two that can't keep their eyes of each other. Pam gets up and joins me dancing. She loves the way the music moves your body... It's how she lost 75 pounds of the past.

She is moving her hips and she is feeling so free. Up jumps the man with the drink in his hand and he wants to dance. So, they all three are dancing in the middle of the room like little school kids in the afternoon... this is too cute.

I go to Sam and I am dancing, and I turn myself around, land my ass right in his pants and begin to get down. I'm all in it like it's free and he is laughing and spanking me... ooh wee! You just a freak!

Pam wants in, she is giggling and comes over to where the heat if hot, jumps in between my ass and the front of Sam's pants and begins to grind. She is all in that! Damn...that's HOT!

Up comes Ms. B and she is laughing and she is gone give her some more, she runs upon her, puts her chest to her chest and begins moving her hips. So, she's dancing there with her breast against her breast, well they are the best...

Sam comes over and begins rubbing up on Pam's booty. Ooh wee!

Pam is game, and she turns around and lets him grind her from the front. It is hot in here and where is my drink? I can't see! So, Sam and Pam are ... hey that's funny, they both only have three letters in their names, too funny... anyway, they are ready to start taking off clothes. Pam asked if it was cool if she did my dude. That's my client and it's my number one rule... we don't screw so we cool!

Sam is easing her blouse open and she is doing the same, the fire is blazing and it's getting hot and the music is driving me insane. Pam runs over and whispers something in my ear... you know I can't hear, dear, what is it? She says, Sam and I both agreed, we are no longer your clients, we are your friends, I last contracted with you over three years ago and Sam just finished, we do business ventures together... you can join in.

It must be the Gin my friend cause what the fuck did she just say? She wants me to join in? I'm still dancing but it changed from getting it on, to a dance of confusion, all the while Sam is dancing with me, cheek to cheek.

Pam comes around to my back and she is wrapping her arms around me and her body close, her head is lying on my shoulder and her pelvis is in my butt. I'm like... WHAT? It feels nice and the flow is slow... I can feel the drinks; my eyes are getting low. I unzip my dress and off come Pam's skirt, she threw on my face, ouch that hurt... flirt!

My cute little panties... My Panties are cute; they are my favorite color PINK... ooh wee! They have ruffles and a cute little bow... I know! (Thanks to my fan from Portland, Oregon... his name is

Santiago G.) They are hell a hot... and my top. My bra is hell a cute too, it's the same color as the panties and the trim is black satin.

I am looking hot and so is Pam. Pam has a lace bra that shows her nipples well, she is looking great over there with the man coming out his pants...My phone rings... as usual.

I answer the phone and it's "the man". We don't see each other anymore but he heard I was in town, wants to check me out if I'm gonna be around.

Can you believe this, that man was the shit... he was my main... ok back to us and this thing that were doing. I got people in my face and they are taking off their clothes, and I don't know what to do so I just move back into with the music moving my feet over to the fireplace.

It's hot in here and the girl is awake... says it's her Birthday! OK! She don't miss a thang...

Anyway... those two over there are hot as hell, Sam's manhood is leading this party and I know how it slangs... it can do some things. Pam is sweating and using her hands to make this person in front of her a man because he is forgetting his in control face, don't make me have to go over there and set him straight. Goodness... Ms. B is looking frustrated!

I walk over there and pull him away as if to play, with his hair and his arms are so firm, I dance him over to me as Pam dances naked alone.

The fire is making sparks and the flames are high, I am whispering in his ear that his game plan is not tight... she has hers down and is making him sweat, but he is showing his weakness. That does not for a great lay make...I mean!

He man's up and gets back in the groove and takes control of his new woman... she is on fire and it's by the hour, she's going to be a new woman. It's getting deep...

Sam is touching her lightly on her skin, as if to tingle her very being. He runs his fingers through her hair, and I stare, from over here. I don't even dare.

I am sipping on my favorite drink; it's green and has me licking my lips. I like what I see but as for me... I don't think for three.
I'm watching my work in action as the two are locking lips...

I taught Sam how to kiss and Ms. Pam can lick some ... let's just say I taught them well! You see, it's all about the Upgrade... If they never got the Upgrade, they could never be this tight.

This is out of sight cause all of Ms. B work is being mixed in motion... we gone have to bottle this shit and sell it for promotion. Ms. B is the shit and it doesn't come cheap. Pam spent well over 50 g's to learn how to sip a dick.

Sam over there with his game recognizing game spent close to 7 g's but learned quick and stepped up slick. That man can slang some dick....

No, it's not all about sex when you get an Upgrade it's about learning to become the man all over again. You haven't been out there in quite a while, things have changed. Your game ain't even the same.

And for you women who say you use to be the shit, well, look down at your clit... It has aged, and your strength may not be the same, you use to be able to throw down and make em holla, but right now you should take some of Summer B's classes to give your legs a chance. These young men these days will wear out your ass.

Don't be playing. Thinking you gone do some stuff and your legs fall asleep, ooh wee!

So, they carry on and I tell them to get a room, they laugh and jump up and reach out their hand, I stand.
I look at my phone, a text flashes from "the man" ... can I see you at 5 in the a.m.?

I stay by the fire, lift my drink to my lips and wave my hand at my friends... go and tear that up, I'm saving mine for the morning as I text Yes to the man.

EROTIC SHORTS TWO

"The Man"

The rain was coming down and it was starting to puddle up... "The man" was on his way to see her. It was four fifty in the morning and she couldn't stand the anticipation.

Her energy is never the same without him. Whenever she feels as if all is lost... "The man" in any form can always rejuvenate Ms. B. It's like Kryptonite; her energy is not the same when the man is not around.

She never was able to understand the reason for this... even asking him if he put voodoo on her one day. Well, I'm just saying.

She is looking out the window and her heart is racing. She has on white tank pajama top and red shorts even though it's raining outside. April showers bring May flowers in Summers world...and "the man".

She see's headlights coming up the driveway... the driveway is long and takes about one minute to arrive at the front door.

When the lights approach closer, she runs out the door with nothing on her toes and her arms are free and it's raining. The car stops, and Ms. B is soaking wet as she arrives at the driver door in time to jump into his arms.

The rain is coming down and Ms. B seems not to care. The rain, it's in her hair. The way the two kiss is like something out of an old school movie. They melt together as if as one. Her tongue is down his throat and he's holding the back of her head so tight. He stands over 6'2 and thick, Ms. B is definitely locked at the lips...

After a few minutes and needing some air, Ms. B backs up and looks in his face. It's raining, and no one seems to notice. Her nipples are showing through her white tee and feet are just as beautiful as when he left. He puts his hand on her face and grabs her hand.

They run inside and laugh as they enter the room. The heat is on and they head for the master bathroom for towels. Once inside, they strip naked and turn on the shower. Let's get nice and warm, it's cold in here.

The man is staring at Ms. B... he misses her smile, he misses her love...

Ms. B is smiling as she checks him out too, he looks pretty cool. She looks up at him and smiles and says, "I miss you".

She takes him by the hand, it's almost six am and damn, I miss this man. So off to the kitchen, cooked up breakfast and sliced some fruits. Ms. B got an idea and pulled out the grapes, jumped up on the island and laid down on her back... The man is looking while he is scrambling the eggs, he is smiling and wondering what is the plan?

Ms. B got the grapes and is placing them down the center of her body with one in her belly. He takes the pan off the stove and washes his hands, well, he is "the man" and he makes his way over to Ms. B who is serving up appetizers.

He is standing next to the island looking down at this beautiful creation that is waiting for him to devour her very being... he walks over to the fridge and pulls out the Cristal Champagne. He opens the bottle with one pop-a-dop.

He pours out a spout right on her breast. Cristal taste best when placed on your chest according to the best sex magazine... All the way down to "the girl" he pours.

Now that the grapes are bathing in Cristal Champagne, it's time to start brunch. "The man" takes his hands and places them behind his back. Ms. B is giggling while the music is playing an erotic beat in the background, its making her heart pound.

He reaches down with his mouth and takes the grape that is at the top of her chest, sips the Cristal. Tingling her nipple as his tongue finds her grace. He takes it all the way until he gets to the girl...

It is hot in this kitchen, and the oven is not on. The grapes are all gone, and the champagne is wet, the girl is so excited that her Big Daddy is back. Once he says hello to the girl, Ms. B wants more. The girl is so excited, she has become so wet. His tongue goes in, his tongue goes out, his tongue wraps all around. Wait ... that's fucking wet. Her thighs are throbbing, and her back is arched.

She lifts and takes him by the hand and leads him to the master suite where the fire is blazing hot. Ms. B is in heaven.

There were a lot of things that the two used to do... he and she shared a lot of first things together as they played in the sand. Back seat in the car was so fun and wicked, the limo, the chair, the kitchen and more. The man was "the man" the missing piece to the puzzle. They fit like a glove when the two were a hit, she wanted to love him, and she didn't want to lose him.

Ms. B is in front of the fire, her skin is glistening, and her hair is wet and curly. The girl just had a trim. Big Daddy hasn't changed one bit. Big Daddy can make the girl do anything he wishes. Pulling out the view master you can see what the man meant to Ms. B. It was something that time didn't allow to be.

The music is playing, and the fire is flickering, the man is standing there holding Ms. B from the back. The heat from the fire is making him sweat. His chin is resting in her hair that is damp. He reaches his hand around to her chest, rubs her skin and her nipples as she leans back into his pelvis. The music is playing, and my heart is beating loud.

SB; Damn I'm wet. Damn he's hard. Damn this fire is hot, can you feel it?
He takes her as she stood. His hand reached for her lip as she nibbled, and he stroked her lips. His other hand on her ass as he lifts her cheeks to peek at the girl at last.
He takes big daddy and rubs a hello. Oh yeah, right there, it's enough crème to make you scream.

He inserts into her very warm cooch ... so juiced. His penis is pulsating at ever stroke. Enlarging as the girl is sucking on him like a popsicle stick in heat.

She slightly bends over as he takes her breast into his hand and squeezes her nipples. His other hand is at her G Spot, how hot while her ass is gently accepting his diligence.
She's moaning, his dick is exploding, and she screams ..." oh shit" as he cums. The two has busted their nuts.
By now it's about seven-thirty and her damn phone rings...

SB; Sure, I can ignore it but with all the business I am in, my phone always wins, damn. It's the hotel and it's an issue with an event. I do not have time for this shit.

If I must come down there someone is getting fired, I specifically addressed this last night with the staff. I told them the man was coming to town and they know damn well how I get down. They gone make me cut somebody.

So, I hang up the phone and look over at my boo, shoot... he so cute! He so understands with all that I do, shoot, he was always too busy too.

I go over to the bed where he is laying his head, staring at my legs as I jump on the spread. He will always be my man. I scoot in and spoon right into his groin; he holds me and whispers in my ear. My naked body is melting into his as the morning hour lingers, and the hotel is on my mind... it's time.

I whisper back...
Lips touched with the softness of her breath... soft as a down pillow and wet as the girl.

Ms. B can win a kissing contest with those lips and she claims to have the pot of gold right there where the girl is the queen of me...

The girl is so excited that Big Daddy is near; she began to shed some tears. She usually doesn't get all worked up but come on, its Big Daddy, and he is the bomb.

Ms. B being the diva that she is never lets them see her sweat, so while the girl may be all excited, Ms. B is keeping her cool. Her hair... perfect, her feet... cute, her hips... slippery and her lips...juicy. I will have to admit, not only is Ms. B the shit, but I can say, and I am sure you will agree that she is the "almost perfect diva, Summer B"!

She has the pot of gold at the end of her rainbow... Well I'm just saying!

The Man is looking into her eyes, trying to understand, how can anyone ever want to leave her? She makes you feel like you are the almost perfect man, she takes care of your every need and she never ask questions or expects monogamy.

The Man will always love Ms. B and she will always love The Man.

He takes his fingers and traces her skin, from her forehead all way down to her naval while taking her to another world with his eyes.

His eyes tell his life story and Ms. B knows it all. You see Ms. B has premonitions and the man's world jumped at Ms. B one day and she began to know him better than he knew himself. There was nothing he could do or say that Ms. B didn't know with her whole heart if it was live or Memorex...

The girl is singing praises to anyone who would listen, and Big Daddy was stroking his yoke. Just like a guy...

The Man is the only one who knows how to love Ms. B. He paid attention while he was in Summer's school of hard knocks. He read a couple of sex books and he tried to watch her, but she doesn't show emotion very much or what she likes. She just does, and you better be paying attention.

Ms. B is laying there staring into his eyes and she is drifting in and out of consciousness as the sound of the rain and the beat of his heart seeps in her skin like the drug of choice in rehab. He makes her feel like her skin is being masturbated and the girl is always in need of a life jacket when she is with big daddy. He is her favorite play date.

It's about that time to get down to the grind and the girl is on fire. What is a girl to do? Well that wasn't really a question...

So "The Man" takes her in his arms and squeezes her tight as he kisses her lips. She will leave you on an island that has only her on it with no clothing, just her lips and that kiss... damn Ms. B, what you gone do to me?

The kiss continues for about five minutes leaving the man very weak and Big Daddy; well let's just say he is quite ready.

The girl gets her groove back when big daddy makes the love attack. He is moving slowly within her walls, as he paints a picture she has yet to see, he is creating a masterpiece. Mona Lisa aint got nothing on Ms. B. Cha Ch'ing is what the girl now sings...sweet!
The man can't believe how mellow sweet she feels, he is at aw at the way she controls him.

No control, in a whole new world, pretending to know what he knows. I don't think so.

Ms. B has him tripping and he doesn't know what to do. He can think of nothing else but to please her. He is losing his mind one stroke at a time and he wonders what will come next.

Like the eagle with pray day after day having a feast on the stray what the hey is that name of that song in my head?

SUMMER BRADSHAU

The man says my name Summer B... I love you! and the look on his face can never be erased from the memory of that moment on this hot and sunny day.

I officially won the race to the ultimate cum face and I laugh really loud and he's confused all the while but he has to laugh too cause my laugh is kind of cute and at that moment in time that my laughter is getting loud the laugh turns to a frown because I too blew a hoot at top of my lungs baby please what's the song that is playing in my head?

Fizzled and annoyed yet filled with joy at the way he just made me feel, that was real. I will love this man forever. But if you tell him I will abort the whole plan... shhhh

EROTIC SHORTS THREE

Pam and Sam

After the man left Ms. B got a call from Pam... it was about ten in the morning the following day.

Pam was smiling from ear to ear, you can hear it through the phone. Ms. B is chuckling from knowing how glowing Ms. Pam must be. Pam tells Ms. B all about her time with Sam...

Sam took control of Pam in the bedroom. The fire was hot and so was his manhood. The two felt the magic that was happening between them.

They were able to slowly feel each other while the music played, and the fire was hot. It was like watching the most romantic love story in action.

Sam was the man and Pam was not playing. They showered and went naked into the kitchen for ice cream... you know what I mean.

They ate ice cream and laughed, and Pam showed him how to enjoy the adult ice cream bar...

Compliments of Ms. B, Pam went to the freezer and pulled out a crystal tray of tiny ice cream balls of different flavors, Ms. B's favorite number... 21.

She led him to the dining room table that was larger than the average bed. It was set with a thick runner for comfort and nothing else. She set the bowl down on the table and climbed up.

He held her hand as she laid herself down while smiling at Sam. Sam was so hard he couldn't stand the anticipation. He was so excited and mesmerized by her boldness.

She took the bowl of ice cream and proceed to place the ice cream on different parts of her body. This was part of her Upgrade back in the day...Cold and wet, her nipples were like glass.

She then told Sam to get the whip cream out of the fridge and place a spout on each scoop. Sam was so happy he skipped over, grabbed the bottle and was back in a flash. Did you see his penis?

He started spouting while smiling and rubbing his man. He started his adventure at the top of her mouth, eating ball, after ball, nipple after nipple, licking till there's none at all. He went back for more. Those nipples were so hard he could hardly breathe.

Pam was so knocked out of this world she could have sworn that she was high. She was seeing double and fantasizing about any and everything.

The sex was so hot, and her body was so on fire, Sam called out her name and she will love him forever... Damn, Sam, you are the man.

They woke up the next morning wondering who and where they were. Sam was elated to have woken up with Pam.

Pam on the other hand, was at first a little nervous. You know... that "I wonder what he thinks of me", nervousness. She was happy but still felt a little awkward. But once they both started interacting with one another, they were like old friends.

They made breakfast and sat out on the deck enjoying the birds and the sun while getting to know one another through stories and laughter. I hope this last... they seem made for each other.

Pam calls Ms. B and she is grinning from ear to ear. Telling her the details of the day and the best part of all was the midnight buffet.

What a treat to hear her laugh and tell the story of love in all the right places. She said the 21-flavor ice cream was a hit and man, can that man lick...

Summer B was laughing because she is the one who hired someone to train him. She knows what he is capable of, but she keeps all of that to herself. You see the rules are that clients are private and unless one asks to be shared with another, no one knows anything about anyone. Ms. B's golden rule.

Pam says that when Sam arrived home, he called and read her a poem. Wanted to take her out tonight to dinner and a play. Sam is going after his woman and he is hitting it straight. It's just the way she likes it. I gave them both some pointers, since I know how they both are you know. It's like if you knew the lotto numbers; would you share the info with others?

Pam tells Ms. B that she will call her after dinner and let her know how it went. She couldn't wait to get into her new dress and her fishnet stockings. Pam is something else.

EROTIC SHORTS FOUR

A Birthday fit for a king

Karen messaged Ms. B a reminder of his birthday. She has done this every year since they first met. Karen does not let Ms. B forget...

It's time to pull it all together Ms. B thinks as she stares into the garden. His birthday is very special to her. She doesn't care where she is in her life... his birthday (sigh)

Born in the same month they are, yet two different beings. Two signs that is so different from one another. Yet... the chemistry between the two is dynamic. With his energy, Ms. B has been known to bring in some high-end clients. Upgrades to the fullest. His energy... allows her to deliver more than she can deliver on her own. Ms. B is a bad ... shut your mouth... but with "the man", Ms. B can rule the world. She never did figure out why this was... it simply was, and they adapted to it over the years.

Karen checked her list of birthday festivities Ms. B put together and made the proper phone calls to ensure all things were in order. Everything must go according to plan or Ms. B will have a conniption fit... what? I'm just saying she will not be very happy.

Ms. B stepped into the limo for the trip to Rosie's Café... almond mocha and a personal shopper to help her pick out the perfect dress for the date with "the man" ... it's his birthday!

Darla, the personal assistant, comes out with a few dresses for Ms. B. When she stepped out of the dressing room with the second dress on, Darla screamed with excitement as Ms. B caught a glimpse in the mirror, she freaking screamed too.

Ms. B is on the phone with Karen, "It is black and up the thigh and the back is open in a circle... the material is silk, and the feeling is so smooth. Feels like a baby's bottom lightly sprinkled with baby powder and my hips feel like sex on the beach in the middle of a flood and the lights reflect my thighs and my heels are feeling high as I sway from side to side oh the feeling that this dress brings makes me feel like... I need to breathe".

Darla twirls Ms. B around as she covers her smile as if to hide the drool that is slipping from her face. From where she stands she is freaking hot... don't touch that button...make you wanna slap your mama! What? I'm just saying!

Yes... I want the dress without looking any further. The dress makes you wanna holler! Summer b.... what you gonna do to me?

The man is preparing for his trip to see Ms. B. He gets nervous this time of the year. The things she does to me he says. She is his favorite girl in the whole wide world and he will always be "the man".

His bag is light as it's a weekend trip, but it is full of everything exciting. A private jet usually starts the day and the rest... you gotta keep your interest. The man and Summer B.... is the shit!

Keep reading!

He steps out into the limo and is taken to the airport in first class. Ms. B is all he can think about and she the same.

She is trying on earrings and giggling as she thinks of him. She looks at the time and gets even more excited. These earrings are perfect, fits my face just right.

The man takes a nap, and, in his sleep, he has a vision of Ms. B a few years back at the Christmas tree. She was decorating as he was cooking, and he remembers her laughter as she tried to reach the top of the Christmas tree with the angle.

The man pulled off his apron and came over to her... from behind he bent down over her neck and kissed her so gently, he grabbed the angle from her hands as he giggled at her on the inside. He loves to see her try things on her own.

She doesn't need a man she says... he is laughing harder as he reaches up to the top of the tree and puts the most beautiful angle into place.

Ms. B, "a reflection of me", she says as she takes him by the hand. Her smile says it all and he takes her by the arms and pulls her close as he kisses her forehead.

Looks into her eyes and places a diamond on her left hand. SHE SCREAMED so loud she knocked over the tree and her fifty-dollar bulb burst into fifty million pieces, but she couldn't even breathe let alone care about the tree when on her finger is a ring that is a symbol of his love for me.

You win... I'm in! But it's only just pretend as they grin, and she looks again at her hand. He will always be her man. The flight attendant announced the plane landing, dreams do end my friend and here we are...

Ms. B just finished getting her hair styled and her toes prepped and polished.

Lunch is light and fast as she rushes to see her man and the smile on her face is that of a canary in a house of spades and back to him... he wipes the sweat off of his hand as he thinks of her plan for his birthday weekend and the fact that she is his girl makes it worth it even more and the cake that comes with it is explicit.

Back at the ranch Karen gets Ms. B ready for "the man". The limo calls in as they are twenty minutes away and the helicopter is waiting for them in the vineyard. Karen looks at Ms. B and is always amazed at how beautiful she looks... like for the first time, over and over again.

The man and Ms. B can never win.... The relationship seemed to be coming to an end. Because they can never be and for her, she needs to catch her wind. The man took Ms. B by storm when he came into her life. As distant as she was, he was the only one that was able to capture her heart. He is the only one that has been able to make her love. They are so great together. He is her missing puzzle piece.

Have you ever made a puzzle with like a thousand pieces and you finally get to the last piece and it is missing? You cannot complete the puzzle without the missing piece.

Like all your hard work has gone to waste. You are devastated, and you feel defeated. Look at how wonderful the rest of the puzzle looks but with the missing piece... oh crap... wwt (what's with that?

Ms. B knows that the man and she will be no more, so this birthday trip will be the last and the sweat on his hands keeps coming fast because all he can imagine is life without her and ... He looks at the itinerary.

The jet takes them to the Hampton's where the beach house awaits. Overnight stay as they play at the Hampton's Inn, the penthouse suite. The jet will then take them to Hawaii for shopping and dinner. New York for a play and back on Monday or maybe even Tuesday.

There is someone on the private jet to give a couple massage complete with fresh fruit and chocolate covered strawberries while sipping Cristal Champagne. She has an autographed ball from the Dallas Cowboys as a gift. A gift from her heart for she knows what he likes. She also has two season tickets for him in the private suite... ooohh wee, birthdays are sweet.

And to top it off, she has a personal text message from the head ... (clearing my throat) in charge of the Dallas Cowboys, Mr. Jerry Jones. "Thank you for being a fan and I look forward to meeting you on our opening day" ...

Did I say Ms. B is the shit... if she likes you, you are in! If not, you better get to stepping. She will chew up and spit you out like bad meat. What? I'm just saying.

His hands are sweating even more. How do you say goodbye, how do you let go? Ms. B is fixing her hair and prancing around in a nervous frenzy. How do you say goodbye, how do you let it end?

The dress is on fire as the mirror catches her flying by. She stopped, doubled back.... Looked at herself, turned to the side and smiled wide. "Damn, you sure look good" she sighed and kept running towards the vineyard to check on the helicopter. Security hustled her over in the golf cart. No problems there, everything is straight, even her lip gloss is flawless. "Oh, I can't wait"!

The limo is seen from the glass plated wall and Ms. B gets excited and can't stop her smile. The limo arrives at her front door and Ms. B is waiting by the back door. The driver opens it and waits as Ms. B stares at what's on the memo…

There is a gift and the memo that reads: I love you too much and can't say good-bye (while he was writing, he was crying). The note is wet as she puts her fingers over it. Her eyes start to swell, and her throat seems to close. Her hand covers her mouth as she grabs the gift and the note. She then closes the door, sends the limo home.

Karen is standing and waiting in anticipation as she sees Ms. B turn around alone and what she sees next brings her heart to the floor… tears are streaming from Ms. B's face. In the years that Karen has worked for Ms. B and through it all that they have been through, Karen has never seen Ms. B cry, especially not like this. She shed a small tear at a funeral. She dabbed a tear at a wedding, but right now, those are tears that are as real as child with no parents. I'm just saying.

Karen is now in tears as she takes the note out of her hand and reads what he has written. I love you too much to say good-bye! Ms. B right now... I wipe her eyes.

Karen calls the helicopter pilot and turn up the lights. Puts the note on the table and put her arms around Ms. B. Come on let's go to the kitchen... I'll make us some tea.

In the lounge Ms. B is staring at the gift. She hands it to Karen and says, "Here, you open this". Ms. B's heart is racing, and she doesn't want to look. Tears are still steaming from her eyes. In one small bag she can almost recognize is a collection of panties.

A note in the bag reads, "From all around the world for my special favorite girl" ... In the second bag was a small box. As she starts to open the box, she looks at her ring that the man had given her some time ago.

It was their secret way of "being married" to each other. You know, in their hearts, in their own little world. He will always be her man and she will always be his girl.

When she was lonely she would look at her ring. When she needed energy, she rubbed her ring, and when she lay in bed at night, she let the ring touch her face as if to bring him close to her.

Ms. B is afraid to open the box, but she does anyway. In the box is a photo of the two of them. She is leaning back into his chest and she is wearing his "Belfry Stetson Hat" she bought him in Italy last summer while he smiles down at her. Also, in the small box is a string... the string was from Paris.

He had given her a string to remember a French word that was hard to learn. She had left it in his suitcase after the trip. He saved it just for her. The last item in the box was a handkerchief. The tag on the handkerchief said "to Ms. Summer Bradshau: may you find peace in my handkerchief, from The Queen" ...

I am staring at the box in awe and the tears are streaming fast. The man had business at hand with the queen and all he can do is think of me and walked out of there with an autographed hanky for Summer B... WTF who does shit like this?

Tears are streaming on Karen's face too! Shoot!

Ms. B grabs the bags and a bottle of Cristal, heads for the bedroom and closes the door. Crawls into bed, opens the bottle...

Karen arrives two days later to find Ms. B still in bed, an empty bottle on the floor and tears still streaming from her eyes. The hotel has been calling and her cell phone ringer is off.

Karen picks up clothes and cups and shakes her head. Ms. B stirs but doesn't awake with the covers hiding her face and the handkerchief in her hand rested on her cheek in her fist as if to never let it go... poor Ms. B closes more than a chapter, it's an end to a sequel.

A few days later ... A personal delivery service arrives at HIS suite with a few birthday gifts

Happy Birthday to my best friend!
(as tears of sadness fall from my face)

The finale of the man... Ms. B will never be the same again

It's been three weeks since Summer Bradshau crawled into bed with a bottle of champagne and a broken heart...

All she can do is sleep and barely eat. The thought of the limo pulling into the driveway and arriving empty was a lot for her to handle. It's like someone died right there at her feet. Karen has made sure she at least ate a cup of soup and water.

Her heart is so heavy that it's hard to function. Like someone pulling you down when you want to stand up.

Having not spoken to him or seen him "the man" has been feeling under the weather as well.

Having had a flu shot seemed not to have helped him. He has not been able to work or eat and his mood is just scary. I love her so much he thinks but his thoughts must stay at home.

Life must go on she says and it's time to rise and shine. It's my birthday week and I need to dance.

Ms. B turns on the stereo player and gets her mood right, calls the hotel and lets them know she is coming in (they love that she does that, gives them a chance to ensure things are straight, she doesn't like surprises lol).

After a long bath and a facial, Ms. B gets dressed and heads out for the day.

Wow it's beautiful out here she yells as the rain hits the top of the car, looking through the sunroof glass at the sky with a smile on her face... life is good, and all the time. Now, let's get this party started!

Where shall she go and what shall she do? Summer B is ready for fun. She is so happy and blessed to have lived another year, why not have fun celebrating with friends and loved ones. And besides, we got another Birthday Story to write... Now... WHO'S MY CHARACTERS?

EROTIC SHORTS FIVE

The Birthday Shower

So, this year's birthday went down like this...

Limo arrived about seven fifteen. I was dressed in a black dress that went slightly above my knees. My heels were about four inches tall.

My hair was curled and pinned up in a sexy and luscious bun that made my face look like it just stepped out of the best spa in Paris.

I am banging if I may say so myself. My heels are cfm's and my attitude is about the same. I am ready to celebrate a great accomplishment.

To live another year is a blessing. If you need a bib, just let me know because I can't downgrade. I can only UPgrade and this is it.

Lifting my glass that is sparkling like my lip-gloss. My lips are nice and soft, and they look a little plump. They have that tasty unbelievable shine that makes you want to suck them like a pork chop bone.

I lick my lips to break the ice. My vice... the limo driver glances back and my dress has risen a tad. My legs are glistening with the lights overhead. I cross my legs slowly... creating heat and tension.

I don't know where we are going. The car arrived with a note that said, 'be ready at seven and wear what's in the box".

I lost myself in bubbles and I hurried into my dream.

I am the birthday queen!
I am laughing in the back of the limo. My aroma is filling the space. Memories can't erase.
We are driving on a windy road and my butt is sliding around. I get excited to know where the limo will go, and my excitement is getting loud.
I sipped on my taste of good cheer searching for the key.

I am the birthday queen!

I feel heat; I feel beads of love falling to the floor as we pull into an oasis I cannot believe what I am seeing. It seems so unreal.

The driver opens the door and reaches for my hand. I am tipsy and feeling rather giddy and I want more. He takes my hand and helps me up to the top of the stoop, there's a door.
The door is open, and the curtains are blowing out into the wind. The driver hands me my bag and he point up to the door. I am trembling with thoughts of what's in store.

I proceed through the curtains to see a fireplace lit. A bear rug and a silver platter with strawberries and cream. There's a note that says, "Love, have a bite of my desire".
I bite into the strawberry and the juice ran down my chin. It's so juicy... so wet... so sweet. My lips are trembling.

In walks the butler with a bottle of champagne... a note that reads, " Love, allow the wetness and bubbles to penetrate your being until I arrive".

I am screaming on the inside. Come on, what the hell. Nobody gets a birthday like this. Am I getting punked or something...

I am sipping champagne and eating sweet strawberries. In walks the butler with a robe and a note that reads, "Love, slip into this robe and wait for me by the fire".

I am like what? I am trembling, and I am misty. I slip out of my dress into the robe, made of silk.

It felt like an orgasm wrapping itself around my body when I put this robe on. It was so silky and creamy.

In walks the butler with a note that reads, "Love, wait for me in the master suite".

I follow the butler as he slowly leads the way. He looks back at me as my breast are slightly moving back and forth as we walk down the hall with the robe swaying open and close for his viewing.

I am the birthday queen, you know what I mean?

I am feeling the sweat between my thighs, moving when I move. I can smell the sweetness that reminds me of love. I arrive at the master suite... I stop and stare as the butler turns to leave.

There's someone sitting there. It's a woman. In a teddy night gown.
I turn to look at the door, but the butler is already free. I look again at the lady.

She is beautiful... Hair up in a bun. Face made tantalizing enough to catch a stare. Breasts are full, and ass looks tight, but wait... what the hell is she doing here right?

I look at the note that is on the nightstand... it reads, "Love, enjoy a taste and see on me".

I look at the woman who is rising to her feet. She looks as if she is about to take total control. I swallow hard as she approaches. What do I do? Do I let her have her way?

I have five seconds to figure it out. I want to let her do what she was told to do to me. I lean back on the chase. My eyes are open wide. My thighs are busting sweat beads like the fourth of July.

I am the birthday queen. I mean...

She takes me by the arm and leads me to the bed. She lays me on my stomach. I look at her not knowing what to do.

I am...

My mouth is hot. My girl is on fire. She puts her knee into my back and I am like what the world is she doing to me. She takes her hands and rubs them down my back... my favorite spot.

How does she know? She smoothly rubs my neck and into my hair. She is in my scalp giving me pleasures of running naked in a daisy field.

Free to be. I have never had such pleasures as these...
I am the birthday queen. But really... what's with the chic?

So... I'm digging it. And I'm in heaven. So far, I am enjoying every moment of the ride.

She takes my leg and she strokes it with oil. Her breasts are moving with the motion of my heartbeat.

I am the fucking birthday queen!

She takes my toes and moves her fingers in between. Back and forth and back and forth. My head is tilted back, and my eyes are closed.

I am...

She tells me its time and she turn me over...

I am now on my back and the heat just rose a notch. She takes my arms and rubs them softly. Gentle. Making circles with her finger tips. Creating an exotic feeling of pulsating rhythms.

She takes her finger tips and dips them in oil. She starts at my neck and works her way down to my breast. The oil makes her hands slip over and over my breast. Rubbing the tension from my chest with her magic oil.

She massages the muscles of the breast and then she massages the nipples. She moves them gently in and out of her fingers... I am on fire by now and cannot be saved.

I am the birthday queen!

She moves to my stomach that is full of sweat. She is stroking and sculpting like a piece of artwork. I am a Picasso between her fingers. She is creating a masterpiece of an illusion. I can be a fantasy and be any dream I wish to be.

Her hands are moving toward my thighs. In between and back again. She moves favorably down my body and back up. She finds my thighs are soft and wet. Wet from anticipation of what may come next.

The heat is making her heart skip a beat. Not knowing what to feel. Is this real?

I am lying on this bed, with my legs weak as noodles. This lady is using her hands as a secret weapon.

Got me mesmerized. All I know is ...

I am the frickin birthday queen

She is working those thighs and my girl starts to throb. She's confused yet at the same time... she's in for the ride.

I feel floored to the bed with the weight of my love, she is rubbing my stomach and she's heading for the girl. I can hear her call out my name... Summer B. what you letting this lady do to me.

She's on the outside of the clit and she knows where the muscle is. She is stroking with the index fingers. Oil allows a soothingly flow. Circle in, circle out, I am about to explode. I mean... my girl! Come on now. I got limits.

I am lying here with my finger in my mouth. She is stroking the girl to no man land. There is no coming back from here.

I can feel her convulsing. I can feel her heat.

The lady is moving up to my breast and back down again. There seems to be an endless supply of oil that seems to overflow. Skin shining, and heat is rising.

I am...

My girl is losing her mind. The muscles around her don't seem to be as tight. She's asking for a lifejacket to help with all the rain. Says she is drowning in my love and I'm about to release the floodgates. My eyes are rolling in the back of my head... Well I am the birthday queen...

She takes my toes and puts them up to her lips. As if to kiss. She lays them gently back down on the bed as I can't take it anymore. My girl is wondering where I am.

Ooh baby...

As the lady in the teddy moves her fingers around my navel, I began to release my love while the tips of her fingers find their way down my thigh. She uses both hands to accept my love. Fingers swirling side by side.

She reaches up as I lay convulsing to the beat of a rhythm I am unfamiliar. Takes my nipples and pulls them between her fingers and release.

I am like, bitch... I'm convulsing. What you trying to do to me...

In walks him, my man, as she hurries and cleans up her mess. I mean my mess.

I am laying there with my mouth in my lap. He walks over to me and examines my body. Dips his fingers in the oil and creates a crazy eight on my chest.

And it happens all over, this time it's for him...

I am the fucking birthday queen, and I am cuming again and again! HAPPY BIRTHDAY TO ME!

EROTIC SHORTS SIX

VALENTINE DAY SURPRISE

So, by now, you know how I get down… I'm happy and carefree and I love being Summer B., right? So, I am at the mall buying a Valentine outfit and I see this handsome man whom I have seen before, in the perfume section. I met him about a year ago at a business conference in San Francisco.

He looks confused so, the nice kind person that I am go over and tell him which one I think smells best. I even go as far as to put some on my wrist and let him smell my scent.

The second time around, he slightly bent at his knees as his face focused on my chest on his way to heaven…

So, I laugh a little and he laughs too and next thing I know I am digging in my purse for a business card. He grabs his wallet out of his pants and writes his cell number on the back of his card and he asks me if I could please be his date for Valentine's Day.

Well you know me; I don't want to disappoint my fans. So, at this point, three days before V day, I got two dates and only one dress. WTF, right?

So, I tell him my dilemma right then and there and he says to me, well let's go over to the dress department and purchase you a dress. So, in my mind I'm like ok, good move but let's see what you're working with right?

We go over to the dress department and he looks me up and down as if you size me up. I stand up tall shoulders back head up. I'm feeling sexy today so ok... let's do this.

I'm smiling, and he is moving his hands through the dresses as if to feel the power that will bolt out of the dress that is for me...

And at that moment that I am watching him, he jumps with excitement as I do the same, the dress in his hand is about to set the room on fire. I am like WHAT! And he is like DAMN! He looked at me and turned me around. I laughed, and I danced like a ballerina. Ok... that was cute.

I run to the dressing room with the sales lady in tow, because you know... (dress cost $460 so she is not letting it out of her site, bitch) (well she started it)

And when I stepped out of that room I can see the entire mall STOP and turn their heads to look at me. It was as if the sky opened and rained money for everyone to enjoy. This dress, it was simply the best.

His jaws tightened up and he walked over to me. He walked all around as if to melt the dress with his x-ray eyes. And I'm smiling because he can't believe it. I mean, I can but ok.

He looks at the sales lady and asks her to wrap the dress in a box. Walks me into the dressing closet (it was huge, but it was for rich people) and puts his finger to my lip and says, "Sunday will be an unforgettable day".

So, he unzips me slowly sliding his finger down my spine. And I quiver. He leaves me to undress alone. As I stand there with this wonder dress half on and half hanging off my shoulders, I see a beautiful woman standing there.

Full of confidence and poise. It's not the body, for the body has its flaws, it's the spirit. Almost the spirit alone. ...

So now it's time to get my groove on!

Step out the dressing room with the sales lady in tow. She is smiling like a canary right now. He takes the bag and grabs my hand and demands more of my time. I am like (in my head), are you kidding me, I got thangs to do.

So, he takes me to the shoe department. (Ooohhhh, I say in my mind) And he walks over to the sexy strappy ones and he holds them up to me.

We look, and we choose, and we act silly trying them on. He's all juiced and I'm pretty cool just having fun. See you at 5 sharp!

...VALENTINES DAY

I wake up in the morning feeling fresh and frisky. I put on my new bra and panties... Red for love. Panties are fitting just right. Cute... you should see!

I have three outfits for the day. My right now, girl you are looking good, I should buy you roses, outfit. Heels to match and the bra is showing slightly as the curve in the shirt dips low. I'm like Whoa...

I have a black strapless dress that is tight and perfect length. Oh, look at my hips. And my tits. Cute...

I have for the finale, a red, hot like fire, tantalizing, mesmerizing powerful piece of fabric that is draped on me like butter and pancakes. Just Ohhh... Damn.... Can you have my baby?

I kick it alone the early part of the day. I go out shopping and had a great time. I hook up with my date number one at about five. I go home shower and change into my G Thang of a dress and the doorbell rings at one past five. I open the door and he is standing there in aww. Can't believe I am who I am and that's really what he saw.

Come in...

IT'S THE LIMO DRIVER

Grab my keys and he grabs my wrap, down the steps into the limo. Limo driver opens the door and inside is the surprise of my life... It's made up look like a room. Has a bed and the bar and loveseat to boot.

There is Crystal at the bar. I slide in and he hands me a glass. It's the best for the lady in the half bad ass dress. I am like what? This is cool, and I'm digging it too.

Drive up north through the mountains and I'm feeling Cristal all up in me. On comes a video that has a man, standing there with a bottle in his hand. Says, baby, lay back and enjoy the plan".

Ok! I got no problem with that. We go through some windy roads. I'm chilling in the bed feeling hot and creamy. You know, steamy. I'm lying on the bed and I see a gift... card reads "nothing more than the best" and the gift... a diamond necklace. Price tag read "Priceless". The driver checks the mirror and he tilts his hat that says, girl you a badass...

So, we stop at a Victorian Inn and out comes a butler that says, waiting inside is a taste of what's in store for you. His hand extended to the open door. I walk in, down the hall, there is a room, I go in. My favorite green apple martini is sitting on the bar. I walk over, pick up the drink and sip...

Out of a door comes this dude and he is hot chocolate, buff arms, chest high and those thighs, my, my ... and what in the name of ... is between his thighs!!!!

He has an iPod and he starts the music with a slow and simple beat, looking at me, dancing my way with his eyes on my mystic. He can see that I'm excited as this drink is going fast.

Sweat is forming, and thighs are burning looking at this son of a gun. I mean damn... don't hurt me!!!!!!!!!!!!

So, he dances, and he moves me to the rhythm of his beat. I no longer can feel my feet. Another drink arrives, and I can hear her scream. "What the hell you doing, this brothers a freak"!

He got me going and I'm high and I feel like crossing the line... boy you better back up off me for I take you to another world... I aint playing!

He sat me in the chair and did a lap dance on my lap. His balls are pretty much slapping my leg. I'm like damnnnnn, all up in this.

Now what the hell is wrong with that? I now feel like I am a man, my balls are blue and in my hand. DAMN!

He grinds slightly touching, so that I can feel his skin and his heat in addition to the beat of the music. He was hot, he was stroking, my mind was soaking wet. His dick was hard, his skin was hot and so was my hands.

I had to see, what all this was about so I touch, and I squeezed, and, in my mind, I begged him please, inject the heat into me.

So, this brother goes on for about fifteen more minutes. I am about to explode. But I don't. Dang it!

As another martini finds its way in my hand, I'm mad. I want my man. So, the man with the leg of a... I mean, the entertainer delivered me to a room filled with roses. Turned and left with a kiss of ambrosia.

My dude called me into the room with the tub, it has bubbles and candles and a whole lot of love. He is sitting there smiling waiting for me to get in... But first ... I gotta pee. I had a lot of bubbly and gin.

So, I'm in and it's hot and it smells good. You can tell he's on fire from the size of his manhood. I'm pretty juiced cause it's more than I expected so I'm like cool! I can do you BOO!

But that's not what good girls do. Aww...

What had happened was... I wanna see my main dude tonight. I can't do two people in the same day. Wtf! I got standards.

So, I peed, jumped in the tub, washed me and him and cuddled for a while. Wrapped it up, had dinner and was out by eight. Sharp!

I shower with my smell good cream. I am ready for my big date with Mr. Big Stuff. This man is hot, and he is lean. He is tall and damn, he is clean. You should see his ass in them jeans. Oooh...

Anyway, I got the dress on and I can't believe my own eyes. I am fly... (That ain't no surprise)

64

I hear the doorbell at nine sharp and I can't wait to open and see who it is. It's Mr. Big. Girl... it's Mr. Big.

If you could see this man... my goodness he is fine. He is about 6'4, 210 and thick thighs. He is the finest dude around. Ass that is perfectly tight. He is fine.................... did I say that already.

He smiles at me and takes my lips and kisses them with his warm and sensuous ones. Tastes like a Popsicle stick. He's slick. Gone pull a move like that.

He is amazed at how beautiful I look. Hell, I done had a shower this morning, a bath with my dude, a shower again... I better look beautiful.

We go to the best restaurant on the outskirts of town. Private room. Four dozen roses and a box with a heart on. I open the box the small card it read, thank you for being my valentine. The gift was ...

Diamond earrings... Man!!!!!!!!!!!!!!!!!!!!!! This nigga gone want some head! Damn... aww just kidding lol

Diamond earrings... a girl's best friend! Perfect size, sat just right. Made me sexy with my diamond necklace. Beauty is what JARED does. (Laughing)

I am happy and give him a rose. What... stop talking... it's in between my toes.
So, I'm calling him to me with the rose and he gets on his knees so that he can accept the rose from my feet, with his mouth. He looks up at me and by now I am all wet inside.... (I said inside)

I grab my glass and chug the rest, I am hot, and I am in pain. This man is all up on me. I feel the same. I'm feeling this. We grab our
65

coats and head out to the car, step into a machine that fits my booty just right.

The seats, tight. The ride, quiet. The vibration, none. What a turn on...

We get to the Bradshau Hotel, Penthouse Suite with a touch of class. This man is about to tap that... ask me no questions and I will tell you no lies.

But for real, look at this place. It is a woman's dream. On the table is a tray of fruit, grapes and whip cream. Damn boy you are good.

We start with the cream and end up with a bath full of bath beads and crystal champagne.

The only way Summer B will fly. (You know I get down with Crystal, but all these baths are gone mess up my hair).

He was able to touch her beautiful soft skin and feel her beautiful face. She in turn embraced his chest with tongue kisses. She gently kissed his nipples with her tongue. Only taking enough yet leaving none. She was able to sit on his lap as he rubbed soap on her back as she gently moved her butt to the commotion. He replied with a thrust almost landed in her butt, but the comeback was that of a playboy book.

Look ... it bounced back in her girl as the shock turned to more, her hands grabbed the side as his thrust became real. She relaxed, as he continued with his man brain on duty, thrusting in and out as she definitely sat this one out until his penis was too large to hold it to itself so he ... grabbed her breast from behind, thrust his penis harder inside and let his cum intertwine with her cress. His penis is pulsating volcano type emissions into her very hot swollen girl now lady.

After we flooded the bathroom floor, we dressed and quickly ran out the door. He drove me over to an empty ballpark, it was dark. I'm like, ok... I'm game.
Then on comes the lights and boy are they bright... damn wtf.

Then on the scoreboard the sign it read, "Happy Valentine's Day" Summer B...

I look, I was juiced. I jumped up and down and looked over at him. Boy, you a trip.

Trying to secure that ...well, you know. Tryna spring a chic.
Then with a boom from the back of the park, outcomes... FIREWORKS!!!!!!!!!!!!!!!!!!!!!!!

You have got to be kidding me. They are red and white with hearts and stripes. They are love and they are pink, they are...
WHAT THE FUCK YOU TRYING TO DO TO ME?
He points to a blanket that lies on the grass, bottle of champagne and two heart shape glass. Bread and oil with vinegar.

There are grapes and chocolate covered strawberries too.
WTF dude?
He lays me down and fed me strawberries as he watches my lips savor the flavor of the night. My eyes are to the sky.

I will never forget this night, for it was a night of everything a girl would dream for Valentine's Day.

As I lay with my eyes on my only true prize, I add this to my list of services...

VALENTINE DAY SURPRISE! It's all about you! And me too!

EROTIC SHORTS SEVEN

Independence Day

By the dawn's early light, she was in the garden picking flowers for her breakfast date. It was the fourth of the July and it was going to be the most exciting day.

Now it catches the gleam of the morning's first beam, and she was smiling and pattering away...

It was after all; Independence Day and it was so much in store for the two. Ooh!

Breakfast is her best meal of the day and she loves to cook it but today is very special...

She has a date!

She ordered a beautiful red white and blue dress that was perfectly formed on her beautiful body and she was so gallantly gleaming.

It was a halter dress that sat right above her knees and her back slightly glistened with gold dust, just like the fairies and her hair rested beautifully on the back of her neck while her legs won the prize for the best of the best.

Sautéed Red onions and bell peppers, garlic and sprouts... fresh tomatoes and greens grown right out back. Red potatoes, Italian sausage, flaky biscuits, the best. Feel the aroma of the seasoning within, while you taste on Crystal orange juice and fresh strawberries and then...

When the car arrived, there were cute little feet skipping to the door, oh what gift of a special kind of love.

When the two encountered each other for the first time in a year, the tears were more than she could spare. She has missed "the man"! Yes, I said "the man"!

In town for a special seminar he decided to attempt to reach her by chance in hopes of simply seeing her beautiful face, his friend.

Once the call was made the voicemail kicked in, the drop of the smile that had clung to his lips now a message of hope that the return of it would win. She is after all, his best friend.

Distance has been the hardest for her as reality must move on. The return of the phone call was a great surprise as she smiled as she dialed just to know she was still loved. After all, he is her best friend...

After laughing and agreeing to a day full of fun, no strings no expectations, just friends having fun. I wonder if she can handle that.

While he dressed for the occasion and remembered her beautiful smile, the pain of losing his best friend made him sit down and ...wondered if he can handle that.

He held her tight as they entered the door that hurt so badly the last time he departed of it. She looked up at him, with her beautiful eyes; her smile always makes me laugh for you can see the sincerity of it all.

She has an award-winning way of making you tingle.... Her happiness is contagious even if you don't agree with it.

Don't worry; they won't happen again... at least that's the plan! Don't be playing!

They make their way to the entertainment room where the fire is lit just a tad, the smell of coffee and fresh orange juice, homemade muffins and cream, what a dream.

He smiles at her and kisses her on her forehead. Remember, she left the man! (It's been about a year)

The breakfast was great the company even greater and a trip to the garden made the day look so bright, he can't wait for the surprise he has for her tonight. Makes him smile harder each time he looks at her. No strings attached! Are you sure?

They take a dip in the pool for a few, look at the beauty of the two... shoot, what they gone do?

He is staring at her as she is swimming towards the other end of the pool. Her ass is perfect and moving about.

His mouth, lip drops, and tongue pops out. Her feet are that of an orgasm on a stick and the way that she breathes always sends you to your knees.

He can't help but to pulsate as he throbs for her being. She swims back and can see this.

He's smiling at her. She can see that he is wanting her. So, she swims into him and takes his trunks off. The water is warm as this section is heated.

She kisses his lips and melts right in... the tongue it wrapped again and again.

She stroked his penis with her right hand, as she chewed his nipple, lightly biting her friend. He was loving this and getting harder by the second and the desire to have a snow day had to wait, a bit much longer.

She proceeded to suck his neck, in an attempt at making her wet, she ventured lower, the water was hot, her stroke was aggressive, the heat was on. What the hell is the name of that song .... as he needs to feel her inch by inch. Boy oh boy ... this is the shit!

They laugh, and they play, and they splash the water away, step out of the pool and separate showers for the two as they change for a trip into town for some fun. Oh, she can't wait for the surprise she has for him, makes her smile even harder as she admires his cute grin. She loves this man... but can't!

It was 11:11 in the morning and they were on their way to see an old movie downtown. What a great way to start the day. After the movie they stopped across the way for ice cream. She loves ice cream on a hot sunny day. He ordered chocolate... his favorite.

By the late afternoon time for lunch for the two and a picnic... how cute. They stop over and grab some sandwiches, potato salad, chips and juice. This is something the two used to do. Cool!

As they sit on the grass enjoying the sun and the fun, they stopped for a moment and look at each other... don't even think about it after she turned her head and he opted for more potato salad... how sad. But hey... this is fun!

Grab that blanket girl and let's make our way out, she has her surprise all lined up and can't wait till 5:01.

The driver takes them on a scenic route, they laugh and enjoy the trip, after all it's the fourth of July and this day is gonna be the shit... don't trip! They got this!

The driver is taking them to a special event, but the man doesn't know this. They arrive at the Grand Hotel and enter with the crowd as they walk in the door, and he wonders what's in store. (His brows have a look of great anticipation and his smile keeps her smile all the while he will not believe it)

It's a private fundraiser for the best of the best, high flaunters and big ballers with the cash that makes their ass stink. Snobby broads, big dick parody, plastic surgery and oh my glory, these people are a mess but it's their money that's the interest. Now back to the gig...

He sees blue and white uniforms, jerseys all signed, big posters and memorabilia and people galore. There was excitement in his eyes as they are seated at their seat. As the coordinator seats them at their table, he shares with them who they will be dining with and to the man's surprise, he was fucking speechless, excuse my French, you know I'm French right?

The fundraiser was for the rich and famous to raise money for a homeless project that she created and that she supports faithfully and one of the main attractions was   The Oakland Raiders and The Dallas Cowboys. The man's favorite teams. Remember the personal birthday gift?

The coordinator stuns him when the names come out of his mouth... owner of the Dallas Cowboys and four of their best. Did you hear what I said... the man is trying to remain from becoming a mess, what the hell kind of shit is this! I love it!

He reaches over and grabs her leg with a tight squeeze, leans into a kiss on her check with a whisper of disbelief... you are something else Summer B! Thank you, sweetie!

Everyone arrives, the meet and greet is great, the photographer captured lots of moments that will never be erased. The man was on cloud nine as they mingled after dinner, autographs, personal photos and badges for back stage.

Back stage was the bomb, drinks and people, food and fun, music, DJs and I don't wanna go home.

It's time for the trip to the stadium where the Cowboys will host the firework display. What a great way to end the day. What he didn't know was there was one more surprise in store... more?

When they arrived at the stadium there were no cars in the parking lot as the car drove them to a private section. He had a puzzled look on his face... she smiled. Walking with an assistant they are escorted to the center of the stadium where there is a perfect display of a private dinner date with beautiful flowers and a gift with a key. It was large and was addressed to the man...he looked at her and smiled again. That's my best friend...

It's the Fourth of July and we're celebrating independence. What a great way to spend the day with a friend that will be to the very last end... Summer B and The Man together again? Ok, wait, somebody trippin!

So, they dine on fine wine, Caviar and a cigar...while the waiters bustle through with dinner for two and the desert was the best, look at those smiles straight happiness. There's special seating for two with blankets as it chills in the night of the stars and the Hennessy aged well in a glass with a toast.

On comes some lights and the Cowboys themselves comes out with the balls throwing all in the air, laughing hard on their way where the couple cheers on. The man is invited to join them as Summer looks on with the biggest smile a girl could ever dream of.

After the play comes to a stay and the handshakes makes their way, the players leave the man with an autographed ball, owner seats for opening day and a sizeable donation to Summers homeless charity and it's not even the man's birthday! What a freaking day! I mean…

The driver takes them to the surprise that the man planned for them, what she doesn't know is that she is in for the … I won't even call it!

The car arrives as the gates open and it drives through a forest of such…. Down to a lake private beach, house is on hit, rented completely for the former Ms.

There are lights on the private beach and lounge chairs for two, drinks with umbrellas and the ultimate horse devour booth. There was her favorite Crystal with glasses fit for a queen just to represent the tenderness of her sweet lips, her lips, are seriously the shit…

In the house is a cook, attendant for two, in the bedroom is the fire and a box with a beautiful bow made of fresh flowers and tulle… oooh that's cute! You!!!!!

The cook finishes as they stare into each other's eyes. They eat a beautiful meal and grab their wine. It's time to intertwine. They sit by the fire on the floor which holds the perfect bear rug, that is thick and oh so erotic. The softness makes you tingle, as the two, becomes one.

He lays her down, he kisses her breast. Her nipples are hard, her girl is getting wet. He sucks slightly and pulls it away, releases back, and does it again. Her breaths are hard, her legs are weak, the girl is yearning, this man's a freak.

He takes his mouth, down to her navel, he takes his tongue, it swirls, it curls.

He finds his way, down to the girl, her legs spred wider, her loves begin to pour.

74

His tongue runs deep, her moans are weak. She thrust her hips, she curls her feet. He wets his lips, comes up for air, sticks his tongue down her mouth again.

The taste of her is on his lips, now intertwined, orgasmic kiss.

He takes big daddy and fills her being. He trusts his hips into deep.

She screams his name, he grabs her hair, she thrust her hips, he touches her there.

She thrust, his dick, her lips, this shit …. Damn… what a trip. The two are hot, the pussy is wet, sucking him back in again and again

He can't take it, he's about to explode, right when, she jumped up …

And like a horse she rode!
That mother fucker like to pass the fuck out!
She fucked the shit out of him …I can't even lie
Rode him like the fourth of July … on a good day, in some hay!

What the hell is the name of that song cause I swear, she done Fucked the shit out the man, that's all I can say!

Her smile is so heavenly when you make her happy and it doesn't take much. She has the spirit of an angle and her inner love is her vise. Captures you all the time! Bam! You're mesmerized.
After they finish love making …

She opens the box and inside is a cute summer dress, white with sequence. Its …damn is all I can think to say, imagine that ass in an Italian design made from her measurements just right… damn that's tight. I'm getting hot just thinking about it.

Her shoes are Louis Vuitton, creamy white pearly beads and cute little stuff the heel high enough as she struts her stuff in the mirror as she looks at him and his smile says it all, when you give your queen the things that bring out the best in her, your reward bigger than any return and her beauty is glowing in a vision of rays that only he can see.

What a fucking day... excuse my French!

There is champagne and dessert waiting at the dock, 10 acres of private land and the beach is off the hook. As the water flows back and forth the air blows her hair, as the split in her dress, makes an open and a close.

Her lips are glistening off the moon and all he can think is ooooh... Me too, shoot!

She leans back on his chest as they sit on a rocker, at the foot of the beach; water perfect, night is poppin. The stars are shining bright in the sky as they laugh and stare into each other eyes... what?

Don't be surprised, back in the day they were the shit, but ... they quit.

As they blanket up and enjoy the music the sound of fireworks starts as she looks around with a startle...what the hell and she smile.

She jumps up and looks at the man and he laugh as he rises, grabs her arms and hugs her tight and says come lay on my lap... he takes her to the lounge chaise for two.

Covers her with the blanket as the stars in the sky become the star-spangled banner from each side, she rose up in amaze and the sky was lit bright and bright all around the entire lake were fireworks in the sky.

They were huge, and they were small, and she was so excited she could not see them all. She spun around and danced with the clouds as the music played in the background.

This went on for a good twenty minutes or so as they held each other tight. He reached down and kissed her brow, aw that use to be his girl.

She is in the highest of highs as she watches the fireworks created just for her, on this spirit filled Independence Day. Yay!

When the last booms are bombed, and the residue finished falling they go over to the table and toast to the friendship of a lifetime.

It's getting late and the driver takes them in town for the final event of the night... her last surprise.

They arrive in the dark at the back of a building her eyes frowned with a half-smile and wonders what's behind the doors... Ha! She gone hit the floor. Ooh wee wait till she sees what's behind door number four.

As they are escorted out of the car with the coordinator the door is opened, and it appears to be dark as they are lead into a beautifully decorated room and wait... is this.... the Louis Vuitton store?

Are you fucking kidding me, there is no one in here but me... oh and the man, ya'll ladies understand.

So, the lights are dim and there is a section over there with seating for six and a bar and a small band. There are lights and a runway as if there is a fashion show, here we go! Grab a champagne glass and a bag with small gifts... what the shit! I am loving this.

He is looking at her smiling and her face hurts from excitement as she keeps her smoothness about her he can feel her squeezing his fingers ... and it hurts!

As they arrive up to the bar where the other four are standing, the waiter hands them glasses and Summer B starts swearing, under her breath as she recognizes who's she greeting... wtf is what comes out, it's the fucking man himself... excuse my French...you know I'm French right?

Back to her and her beautiful demeanor greets the man as if she's pleased not freaking. Louis Vuitton and an assistant or two, in a private show created just for her...SOMEBODY PINCH ME!!!!

They talk and laugh, and the show begins as they take their stands and what an awesome end to a great day. The show was a hit and the next thing that she was hit with was a list ... you know, of what she wants to purchase...and I'm not gone even say it!

Ok... I can't help it... that fucking list excuse my French was unlimited! I can't even believe it. As my grandma say, shit on that shit! And she ain't got to pay a dime... it's all on the man and Mr. Louis Vuitton!

There were about ten outfits that were displayed; all had handbags, shoes and accessories. Can somebody tell me what is going on, I look at the man with that smirk on his face because he knows he has pulled the ultimate display of his love for Summer B.

Summer B is humble and sweet, doesn't spend a lot of money on useless things, and to be honest, she's not that girly and she really has just begun to wear cute skirts and puts some high heels on, so this... This is the bomb.

So... what did she get? About three-fourths of it. That was a trip. They had drinks and took photos had a video for future proof, that those shoes she was wearing was personally autographed and waterproofed… oooh, HAPPY INDEPENDENCE DAY home of the free and land of the brave!

Wait till you see her at the next event… in her Louis Vuitton chic showdown outfit… better get your glasses fixed!

You think Summer and the man gone be able to end this? I'm just saying!

EROTIC SHORTS EIGHT

The Pot of Gold Under My Rainbow

It was raining outside, and Summer B was heading to the Bradshau Hotel. It was Monday and she had work to do. Seven o'clock in the morning and she was feeling rather fresh.

Her new short do is sexy too... ooohhh!

Ms. B felt a ting of swanky and wanted a new look.

She called Leroy over at Salon Manaz and told him about her itch... he smiled and dialed and hooked her up with Tone.

Tone is the best stylist on his block, he can make Whoopi look like she has a .... The magic wand in hand my friend made Ms. B look young again. If you thought she was happy before... somebody better, ask somebody because she is dropping em on the floor.

When Ms. B passed Leroy at Prada the next day, he didn't even realize who was in his eyes. Ms. B winked, and he smiled, browsed, Ms. B laughed so hard she caused a stir. Leroy heard her voice and stared in her face, Summer B, he backed one leg up with his eyes out of his head and a look of disbelief, oohh weee, Summer B you must be kidding!

Everyone was looking around wondering what's all the fuss about... they were admiring the beauty of the beautiful stature that had walked in the door, full of grace and poise and now she is on the floor, laughing her butt off.

Leroy walks over and laughs at her too admiring the pulchritudinous woman, words cannot even form; Tone on his speed dial happily fills him in....

I did the research on her personality and the work that she does, watched her laugh, seen her play and was in awe the way she handles the hotel each day. From her profile and her being I came up with three cuts and colors.

Gave her some curls and called the makeup artist in, Leroy please, you know why they call me the next best thing to the .... I gotta go I'm trimming the mayor and he is walking in the door. Laughing all the way to the bank Tone is a bad ass and as a personal stylist he is the shit.

Ms. B is feeling rather sweet about her new Upgrade. She is runway model gorgeous and got step it up status within.

When she walked into the hotel, everyone paused... who is that just walked in the door.

Wearing a look of control in your eyes you do follow step by step breath by breath as she sways this way and that, hair is bouncing, short and stout, bitch ass Sassy in tow on her Louis leash, legs spark your eyes and her feet takes you in... you are weak on your knees and your thoughts pull you through back to me and my eyes elevator opens tongue feels like glue... whew!

Was that Ms. B? You must be kidding me!

She said she was doing herself an Upgrade, but an invasion of a body snatchers was another thing, I gotta call Leroy Melanie yells out and runs to call her friends.

Ms. B is happy as can be and is ready to get to work. Although right now, she's horny. Yeah, as she states in her book Purgatory Living, a new look can get you new dick but her new client is on his way in. Upgrade, male, CEO of something (worth millions) and he wants to marry his best friend. So... we do the Upgrade on both and create a fantasy wedding. In the meantime, Ms. B gets a phone call from a friend...

Looking at the clock Ms. B has a date. The limo is scheduled to pick her up at 10 a.m. Something about a taste and see. Sounds like fun to me, I am in. So, the limo arrived promptly at ten. She made her way down the elevator and when the elevator arrived from the penthouse suite they were waiting to see if they see what they saw or was somebody tripping.

Ms. B is laughing because she knows they are freaking out about her new look. They are all talking at the same time and are loving the pulchritudinous woman who stands at their feet. She thanks them all and buys them all lunch as she heads for the limo wondering what's in store...

Inside the limo sits a card with a glass of Cristal... her favorite and it reads; I understand the surprise and you may need something more fitting for your day out, so you are on your way to Rosie's Boutique.

Are you kidding me? Ok.... No need to say more. I am smiling and drinking my Cristal belly up and the temperature is rising high. I am in Summer's World!

Inside Rosie's awaits sparkling water with a touch of fresh lemon and a personal shopping consultant.

I love it when I have arrived. We find the perfect cute skirt and cute little sandals, this is for the trip to the day spa, the note read.

The day spa... ok so he trying to dig a chic. Ok I'm in... Off to the day spa the limo driver is smiling. She stepped back into the limo looking flyer than the runway model and a split that goes up to the vagina ... well, fancy that.

82

There at the day spa Mr. Chin awaits Ms. B's arrival. A personal touch for an exceptional woman. Mr. Chin only serves the best of the best and Ms. B has him all taken in.
She gets a mani and Pedi and feeling so hot when she stepped into the spot. Mr. Chin pulled out no stops. By the time Ms. B finished she was weak as noodles... I mean weak...like...noodles....

The note in the limo reads... you should now be ready for me...

Looking like the perfect shade of brown on her tannish vanilla skin. She stepped out of the limo in a skirt that was to die for. Walking with a sensual step in her path to ecstasy.

He is waiting in anticipation at what creation will take him away. Anytime he gets swept into Summer's world it is worth every bit of the wait.

He can feel her heat as she approaches the room, eyes closed, nose open in a whole other world, take me back to when life was good, feel my love feel for you...

She takes her fingers and runs them through that gorgeous lock of hair, they dare to stare. Ms. B sways over to where he stands, and behold, it's Lane from Rancho Cordova.

His eyes were excited, and they joined hands, the two are friends. He has a bag in his hand as he wraps his arms around her.

The mistress of the winery guides them to a private room. Waiting for her is like a dream. Cristal Champagne, chocolate covered strawberries... you know!

The room is all white and the flow from the windows, the bed looks like pillows and the table is set for two, the decor is that of a beautiful honeymoon score and I'm like whoa...

But I'm down and It's breezy as the wind from the room brushes my hair close to his lips, as he smiles a smile that is fit for a king, in front of him if only for one day is the woman he crowned his queen.

What's in the bag? Need I ask...

The first is a small box and it's blue from Tiffany's. Cute little diamond earrings, my favorite thing. The second little box was personalized for me; Summer B... inside of the tissue were the cutest little panties one would ever see. Rainbow... ooh wee. A colorful delight and a pleasurable twist, Summer B is gonna write a story in this... ok that's different.

I love these panties, they are as can be, oohh weee Summer B... what you gonna do with me?

Outside of the room awaits a horse-drawn carriage... a perfect ride for the perfect girl. Her hair is blowing in the summer breeze. Inside the carriage is a blanket for the two. Scoot on over girl, I'm gone sit all up under you.

The carriage takes them on a wine tasting tour, inside this one and that one with the taste buds a clapping at the different aroma's coming from each glass. I'm gone have to spank that... ask me no questions and right now I can tell you no lies.

This wine tasting cellar is private just for the two. Ooh. There are grapes and cheese on the table. There is sparkling water (her favorite he listens) and over there is small cubes of ice, her vice. Up her cheek and around her back, it's wet. Smell the scent of the wine that is poured down her lips, and kiss.

Her diamond earrings reflect the beauty she already entails, and her panties under that white dress, she is the shit.... Did I say she is the shit, I mean really, all I can see from here is rainbow underwear. I swear, what the hell. Just beauty and you know the rest...
Ok, back to the story!

Her sandals show off her feet and her toes are glowing. The sun on her face makes you wonder. Would she ever want just me, or will she forever be the freely Summer B? I want her... to want me...

They sit at the table and they share an open glass. He feeds her cheese and she is now sitting on his lap. Over there on the cot that is made for the two, she lies on his chest while the music plays tune. Hear her heartbeat, hear her heart, beat…. Hear her… heart… beat! Now breathe… whew

Her smile is wide as she enjoys her lovely day….
The ride back to the chosen winery is beautiful. The sun is making its way to rest. Her sunglasses sit perfectly on her cute little nose and her smile is showing. He has his broad shoulder look of satisfaction as he watches his girl wrapped in the blanket with her nose slightly cold and my fingers wrapped around her toes. They step out of the carriage where the host awaits them.

Dinner is now served near the private room for two… ooh. I just love this man, he is doing all that he can and his plan… wow. Make me wanna date again.
As they enter the vineyard, there is a blanket rested under a vine. The smell of the vines is the perfume of summer in the valley, breathtaking at best. The ground is slightly damp in the shade from the rain the night before. The heat from the day is drying it all away but for the moment, puddles stay.
As they eat the dinner that is fitting enough, eyes roll back, breeze comes through and a sigh of happiness comes. Ms. B is captivated by all of this, walking hand in hand through the vines as the sunsets and the moon glistens. The stars shine bright if only for one night…
As they lay in the basking of the day and the night, Lane makes a move for the pot of gold under my rainbow.

POETRY IN MOTION

(random poetry)

The mystic shower

(grab your bib)

The steam was on the mirror when she undressed. Skirt that sat right below her knee is now at her ankles. Her underwear is lace and has a bow on the back with a rhinestone initial. S B

The steam is filling the room as she moves onto her shirt. She lifts it over her head with a thrust of a pull.

Her boobs are moving from side to side as she struggles as the shirt is a tight shirt. Sat on her like a snake's skin. Smooth and silky yet rough and desired.

She gets the shirt off and it is now on the floor. Her bra matches her panties and her nipples are showing through the lace. She looks through the steam to admire her beauty.

She turns to the back and checks her ass. It's perfect she thinks as she rubs her hand over.

She pulls the panties down to her ankles and she steps out of them. She admires herself as she moves towards her bra. She unhooked the bra from behind as she turns this way and that way admiring herself in the steamy mirror. She likes what she sees.

She pulls off the bra as if in front of a camera and wipes the steam from the mirror. She is beautiful because she wants to be beautiful... not because of how she looks, but how she feels. She creates her own beauty.

She steps into the shower and the steam is really flowing. In the shower... hands wrap around her waist to move her closer. The water is hot and hard, and the steam is thick. There is a fan that is going somewhere but you cannot tell. It is HOT in here...

He grabs her ass and pulls her in and her belly touches his belly. The water is hot, and the steam is thick...

Water is falling over her face. She is breathing heavy as their lips touch. His hands are digging deeper into her skin as he holds her ever so close. There are no words. There are no sounds. Just the water... trickling down...trickling down. Through their lips, and over her thighs. It's hot as hell and the steam is thick.

He leans her against the wall and holds her hands up and against... she is not objecting to any of this.

He is leaning in and tasting her neck with his body into her body as the water trickles in. Where is your life jacket, I don't think I can swim...?

He turns her around and in front with her ass against his stomach. Her head leaned back on his chest and her hands are explorers. He grabs the soap and he squeezes it on her boobs and rubs it in. Her back is in his manhood and her hands are ejaculating the soap in her hands, so she can wash all her skin.

It's hot in here and the steam is thick. The bathroom décor is very sheik and impressive... bachelor colors yet inviting and tantalizing. He is rubbing the soap on her chest down her leg. She is leaning her head back into the water as it runs all down her face and into her girl... touch her here touch her there and with every touch comes ...sounds of pleasure.

Turn me around, run your fingers through my hair, and oh don't forget to touch me over there...

He takes her hair into his hands and runs them through as the water separates the strands. He is staring into her eyes as the water trickles down...

He is about to explode. The water is hot, and the steam is thick...

She takes the soap and she lathers him up and her hands are sliding up and down and around real slow. Her hands are slowly sliding onto his stomach. She is making circles as her fingers go round his naval. He is staring in disbelief that anything this trivial could feel so good.

She was staring into his eyes while her fingers went down his leg. She rubbed circles around his knee and down to his feet. She squatted down as she took his foot and massaged it as she cleaned and moved on to the next.

She washed her man...

Her hands were all over him. She turned him around and rubbed soap on his back. Moving slowly, making her way down to his butt. His butt was nicely built. Had the perfect shape and thickness. Enough to make a pair of jeans sing. His ass was tight...

Her fingers moved slowly over his neck and around to his chest. She is going for Big Daddy the girl hears her name. Big Daddy, feels the same.

The shower is freaking hot and the steam is too damn thick...

Her lips are trembling as he turns around and grabs her head and takes over her lips. Her hands are around his...

Breathe girl... breathe... its hot as hell.

Her leg finds its way up to the wall of the tub to allow the girl to be able to breathe a little, while getting a massage.

So... her leg up high and the soap is being applied. The water is hot, and the steam is thick, and the girl is down with this rub a dub shit. Are you kidding me?
His fingers go inside and comes back out. She's about to die.

Her head is hanging down because she can't take too much more. She turns around grabs the towel and heads for the door. He is like whoa...

Back that ass up...

Grabs her hand and turns her around, lifts her back into the shower. She is laughing, and he is too while he kisses her boobs. Oh, how he loves to kiss her boobs. They are soft and sweet. They remind me of me...

So, he is kissing her so hard and it's deep in her throat. She loves the way he kisses her. She is moaning and moving her lips over here over there and it's hot and wet. They can win a prize in the kissing contest. They are Hot! WTF?

She turns her head to the shower spout opens her mouth and lets the water run in and out again. He is behind her playing in her hair. Making her moan with pleasure. The water is hot, and the steam is thick. This is gone be some shit... excuse my French!

Rub your hand down my spine and feel my body shimmer. Boy... I think we got us a winner. I mean damn, this dude is hot, and he knows just what to do. He aint no fool. Shoot...
I got skills, but this dude done let the smooth taste fool him. I turn around; take his manhood in my hand... I made a friend.
Introduced myself to the twins, we became good friends. Had the knees reaching the floor, oh how he wanted more....
Did I say, "the water is hot, and the steam is thick"?

The mystic shower brought sounds of love… sounds of desire… sounds of… the untold!

When the door opened for the first time, steam rushed out into the rest of the place. Out walked beauty and the beast.

Summer B… and the Mystic Shower… boy that was that HOT and the steam was thick… Gone make you wanna marry that chic.

But remember … ***Don't Let The Smooth Taste Fool You!***

Penetrate My Soul

As you lay... your thoughts are of me
You lay next to me it's 5 am, my favorite time of the morning
My body is warm, and the steam is light, the creme of my desire
You look over at me as I sleep, in your mind .... my eyes .... you can see
How amazing you are to me, every time I look at you
My heart skips a beat...you are the reason I breathe
My lips ... you touch with your fingertip
I stir ...
I moan .... its 5am and the bed is warm
With my lips your fantasy about every kiss, as they melt within your being
My lips make you wanna scream, I stir...the bed is warm
My nose .... you smooth the touch as so gentle
The site as a cute button be, amazing to love me
You smile as I stir, and your vision go to me
As we swim in the seven seas, you are my everything
In your mind ...I can be anything you need me to be!
Penetrate my soul ... as I sleep

Monday Night With Me

It's Monday night and the bed is turned down as I slip into my gown.
My thoughts are of you ... last year around this time, my birthday was near.

You were the very one to whisper happy birthday in my ear
Your soft breath your soft touch enlightened with my glow.
I can smell your skin ... I can feel your love flow.

As I now get into bed, I am reminded of the way you touched me.
And the way you held me so tight ... (my breaths are getting deep).
You gently stroked your fingers oh so lightly over my body as if to heal.
Yet the oil was warm in your hand, and the girl .... Well, she's a fan.

As I lay here, heart skipping a beat, thinking about the things you use to do to me.

The sweetest fruits and the chocolate kisses ... made me want to be your Mrs.

My heart is now in high command and the girl is not far from there.
I miss your touch and I miss your kiss.
The girl sends her love, says she daddy she does miss.
My eyes are falling into the abyss with my last thoughts of this ....

My back was arched, and the fire was hot on the Persian rug in the loft, you were in and out.

I was round about and the two were so intertwined then … our love …. (Wait stop) …. (It's getting hot) … Our love melted …. Our love melted …. Into …. One!

It's Monday night and you thought football was all that you get

I'm Summer B … your poetic mistress

The Fairytale Begins...

Imagine long legs that seem to fall into place as they sway back and forth unto you upon the arrival.

I felt something in my heart for the first time, it skipped a beat, visions of her danced and pranced as I reminisced.

Sultry eyes and a stature so pure, silk satin creamy flavor, penetrating style and that pouty smile

She touched my arm and my heart she then won, it was pounding and pounding I was losing my mind

Lips to my ear in a whisper of a sound, no stockings on her feet and the scent of her love

I was ejecting beads of mist on the palms of my hands, as my mouth opened wide to express my claim

She whispered, "My love for you is running down my thighs

I am in the penthouse suite, bathing in crystal champagne. They will deliver chocolate covered strawberries and a can of whip cream

I will expect you to arrive in a few, let me give you a picture of the art that's in store for you" ...

She opened her coat, inside caramel skin, lace and satin and a body that makes your head spin.

Off into the elevator she went as I watched from the cloud I was on up to the top, button red and on the P, penthouse suite... my heart skipped a beat.

I asked for a drink, swiped my lips, fixed my pants, fingers flow through my hair to be a man.

Heading towards the elevator door, push the button and it opens as my heart pounds harder.

I think people can hear, " in a bath of crystal and a can of whip cream" ... my phone rings.

I'm sweating faster than a pig in a pen, manhood directing my steps and the phone keeps ringing.

Elevator door begins to close and I'm looking at the screen caller id says it's the wife, you gotta pick up the kids at three.

You look at the buttons that's waiting for you to push P, you push the button that says open.

Step out into the lobby of the hotel, look back at the elevator door as you drop your head onto the floor.

It seems as if time has stood still, lost in the fairytale of the unreal...

Man up and come again!

The cigar room at The Bradshau Hotel

Sitting in the cigar room of The Bradshau Hotel, chase lounge, glass walls, glass of Hennessey, legs crossed side by side. evening gown drops off my shoulder, my shoes says, "come fuck me" and in walks... You

With my cigar lit... I ask, "would you like a light"?
Flicked my lighter, sparked to flame, as my hair falls forward.

My eyes meet your eyes as they lock into a stare, I can hear your heartbeat from here.
So now your sweating and your chest is on the rise, my nose touches yours in a speckle of a moment as I whisper in your ear.

Your leg jumps as if it were on cue... lucky you. You look startled as you try to explain sweat on your forehead and mine up my leg, the cigars are all lit, I lay back with a smile.
your standing there choking with a hella of a hard on.

I stand up, walk over as I push up my boobs, staring into your eyes you don't know what to do.
My hips go left, and they eventually swing right, my feet in sequin my dress is tight.
My face is flawless, and my scent is just for you, my finger on your lip, creating silence with your spit, you stand there waiting and your heart is getting loud.
I push you onto the chase and walk off, after I exit the room, drop the cig in the can.
turn to look again...

SUMMER BRADSHAU

There you are, lying there in awe, wishing you can have all that you saw.

Do come again my friend!

Its morning ....

Anticipating your arrival as I look at the clock. My skin is under the blanket and its nice and warm, soft to the touch.

As I lay there thinking of you my mind is full of memories. Our last encounter was one of the few. We lit the fire as the fire is lit now.

I lay on the fur rug as you rubbed my back with lavender oil. As the heat from the fire melted my skin, your fingers dig deeper within.

As your strokes got more rapid and my skin was warm and buttery, your heartbeat began to get louder, and the girl began to call your name.

The warm touch your warm kiss your tight embrace ... amazing.

As I lay back with my eyes closed I can feel the fire on my skin, as my body squirms with desire, that night on the fur rug makes me perspire.

As I lay here in heat thinking of you, the fire crinkles in the back ground and the girl is tingling wildly as my lips separate in awe...

My back arches as my memories go to you and the anticipation of your arrival. What's more amazing is ... you're coming from nowhere special... just work. But every time you're gone, I want you even more!

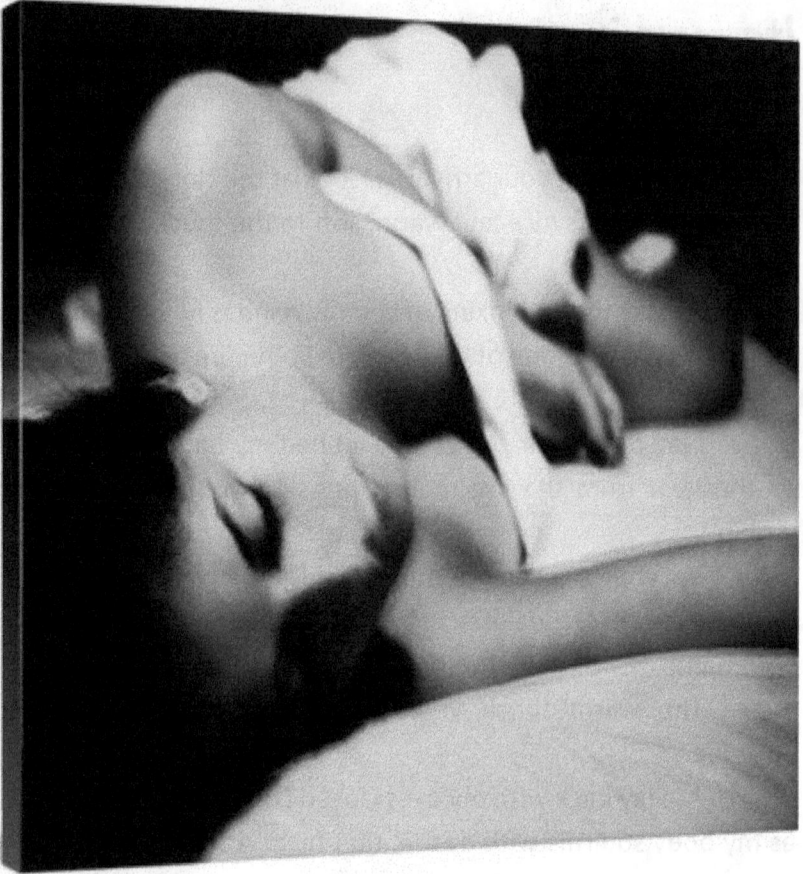

Rainy Night Thoughts

AD LIB; she was waiting for me in front of the coffee shop... it was raining. Her umbrella was a beautiful reflection of her inner being. She was dressed, rather lovely in her skirt and rain boots. When I stepped out of the cab she stepped up to greet me. Excited, she threw down the umbrella, stood on one foot with the other behind her, wrapped her arms around me as she is getting wet, kissing my lips like never as my heart stops .... (the thought you get when you see her from inside the cab through your window, for you ... don't even know who she is but as beautiful as she looks, you can't help but to dream)

SUMMER BRADSHAU

We Swam Inside The Earth's Tears

Sitting here thinking of you on this beautiful crisp night. The moon is hitting my skin just right as my eyes slightly close and my head is tilted back.

I can smell your scent and its taking me way back... back to the day when you took me by the hand, led me to the beach in the sensual warm sand and my heart it skipped ten beats at the touch of your skin as we jumped inside the water, hand by hand, we swam inside earth's tears.
Naked!

The Apple of My Eyes

Green Apple Martini's looking pretty
Calling my Name

Once you have a sip of me,
girl you will never be the same

Nice and sweet, lick my lips
 and the brim of the glass

Feeling sexy, it's Friday Night
On the dance floor shaking my Ass

The sweetness penetrates my soul
As the glass is replaced by another

The face on that brother is looking better and better
Girl, you better have another

Music is bumpin DJ is fine
Someone is watching from across the line

The Apple in my eye
Lips get locked, lip gloss replaced

Sticky and capable of putting me under
I feel the heat from my feet rising high
Sounds like THUNDER

Somebody from across the room

SUMMER BRADSHAU

Looks like he's stalking
Look like he's cute

Green Apple Martini's called out my name...
Once I took a sip, I was never the same
My lips got sticky and he liked it!

Would you...

Would you take me as your wife?
Love me solely unto you...
Fearing nor forsaking what I feel, you feel it too!

Keep me closely to your heart, feel mine beat the same as yours.
Breathing my aroma and drifting into space...
Would you sweep me off my feet? Share your life with only me? Will you catch me when I fall? Would you?

Would I be your only Queen? Give me diamonds and not just rings?
Would you let me share your pillow?
Wear your socks and share your drawer? Would you love me more and more? Would you?

If I give you everything, love only unto you, Make you my **KING!**
Rub your back when you get in, cook your dinner and chill your Gin!
Make you feel like you never felt before, from your head down to your toes!
Loving you more and more...
If I satisfy your every breath-taking need, bathe you and keep you warm... Allow you to be as free as you need to be ... Will you marry and love only me?
Feeding you pleasure on a popsicle stick.
Making your fantasy very realistic. Listening to your desires, keeping the fireplace flowing with hot embers and chocolate kisses!
Would you take me as your wife? Would you?

See you done messed around and ...

SUMMER BRADSHAU

LET THE SMOOTH TASTE FOOL YOU!

YOU can't marry the FIVE-MINUTE FANTASY GIRL!
(read the BLOG: Your Five-Minute Fantasy)

She will eat you and spit you out like some bad meat. Take the fantasy
and keep it moving and finally, keep my motto close to your heart:

"DONT LET MY SMOOTH TASTE FOOL YOU!"
I'm googable... google me... ooohh that tickles

¿

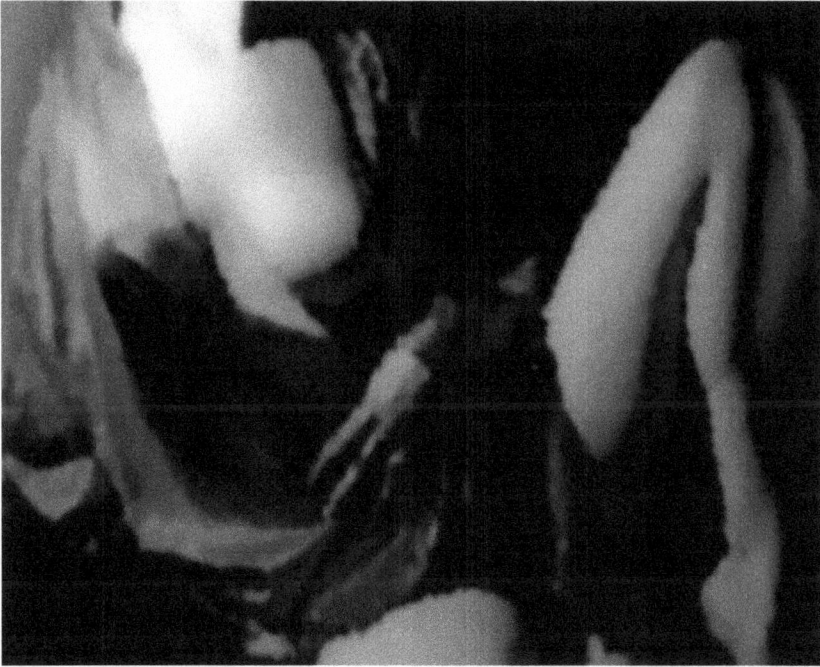

5 Minute Fantasy

At the stroke of midnight, I become your five-minute fantasy
The smell of my perfume and the scent of my being
Caramel skin and pretty brown eyes
Satin touch with the perfect melting lips .... Mesmerized

Lust beholds you, unfolds you into a fantasy
A vision of a masterpiece created by you
Sassy legs sway in with this beautiful creation

Imaginary sets in as my body shifts into stature
Eyes roll back into the top of your head as you watch
You sigh a sigh that no one else can hear

SUMMER BRADSHAU

Pretty face, pouty style and enough sunshine to make you smile
Is this imaginary or could it be real
Putting into place the remarkable desire
Wanting the prize before the race, saving grace
Is this all an illusion claiming your fate
Fantasy or love long waited for ...

Breathe in the aroma of my heat
Watch me proprietor the scene and let it take you into control

You don't resist and follow down the winding way
Where the wind blows slightly by your ear

Hear my heartbeat with each breath
Lips throb with each motion
And you start to sweat as you take it all in

I am, Your Five-Minute Fantasy
Come again!

In Too Deep

Looking out the window on a beautiful warm day
Watching him swim across the pool
His chest so firm yet smooth to the touch
His arms so manly yet melts with each embrace
His legs, powerful yet bends at my feet
As the water overtakes the breathtaking air I can feel his touch from here
I step out of my dress, out the door I go
As I step my feet into the pool his eyes meet mine
He continues his stroke, I continue stepping in ....
My legs sway this way and that way as I find my way into the abyss. can you imagine this ...
When he swims back my way, he stays and down under he goes as I wiggle my toes and up for air, the girl is hot down there yet the water
Surrounds my nipples
I am in too deep and so is your pulse!

SUMMER BRADSHAU

Imagine Me

Close your eyes and imagine... Me!
I'm walking in the room, it's hot outside
My lips are beaded with sweat
See my breast moist at the dip
And my neck is looking rather tasty
I can feel your heart beat....
The air is on and over there
As it blows with a coolness about it
I walk to the bar, order my drink
As I wipe my lip with my finger tip
Its' hot as hell and my mouth is dry
I can feel your breath from here
Feeling mighty hot
The bar tender smiles and doesn't take my cash
The man at the end bought the drink
I tip my hat thanks for the peppermint jack
Back to me... you see I'm on fire!
The split in my dress goes to the highest
And my shirt is as low as it goes
But so nice and well put with that lace at my hip
And did I say it's hot in here?
With it cooling off a bit
You can see sweat on my tits
As I walk to the air over there on the floor
Dress blows up as my head turns in
Ice cream songs for the melting of my girl
And then I twirl to the beat of your heart
I can feel the beat from my heat pulsate your mind
As the air is blowing and I rub all over my body

EROTIC SHOWERS

It's hot but the glass on my chest cold with ice how nice
I finish my drink and I can see you drooling!
My skirt is blowing in the air as so is my hair
I lick my lips and walk away
Drop the glass on the bar
Tip the tender a ten
Walking over to you as you stare into my boobs
My lips are being licked as the heat makes my legs stick
And your heart starts beating faster as my pace is hot and heavy
To your lap in front I stand as your manhood overtakes you
I grab my dick and wipe my chin
Walk out the door, you hit the floor
Come back and see me again …. My friend!

"I MISS YOU"

(THE PENIS OR THE PUSSY)

When your EX says, "I miss you"! what that really means: MTP

"I miss you"! No, you don't miss me, you just miss the pussy/penis **#IMTP**

People say those words all the time …. "I MISS YOU" … do they really mean it or is it that they really just miss the sex you had?

Missing The Pussy or Missing The Penis, either way it's gonna be missed! Why is it that the best pussy or penis in the world is usually not your forever, but your seasonal pussy or penis?

I mean the kind of pussy or penis that is "OMG" good. Never have to worry about deflation, motivation or deprivation. Just always, OMG good! Yeah, well, just know its seasonal if indeed its seasonal and keep it moving. One thing one must never do is "MISS THE PUSSY" or "MISS THE PENIS"!

Sure, one day you will be driving down the street and suddenly you get one of those "OMG" feelings that makes your body shiver and quiver. Surely one day you will be sitting in a waiting room full of people when you get that "OMG" feeling that makes you close your eyes for a brief second, moan out load (as you hear yourself moan you open your eyes and see that everyone is looking at you, so you say "my back is hurting so bad, omg" lol).

Relationships that don't last often has the best sex tally. Don't mistake love for great sex. Often times when you get caught up in the great sex you may blurt out that you love the other person because goodness the sex is so good, you actually could love them and right now while you are screaming their name it may seem natural to blurt out the words, "I love you" when in fact it's the pussy or the penis that you are really saying I love you to for the person on the other end, is just, great sex…. sorry to burst your bubble boo but know the difference and know your role!

The relationship may be fun and exciting, you do lots of things and have great things in common but … there is one thing that is truly missing… the real love. For the real love was not meant for you to have. The sex is what made chemistry, made babies, made cum, made smiles, made issues etc. The sex was the motivator whether the body was present or not. So please sir/madam don't get it twisted.

Often when you are laying on the bed, thinking naughty thoughts and looking at old pictures, please know, the "miss you" feeling you get is simply missing the pussy or penis, not the person. You are missing that "OMG" feeling you used to get during and after sex. The kind that can call you back 20 years later like it was yesterday.

Please dear friends keep my motto at heart: DO NOT LET THE SMOOTH TASTE FOOL YOU! it's just your hormones speaking to you in the dark. You are not missing that person you are missing that pussy. You are missing that penis!

Don't make the mistake to reclaim the pussy or penis. In doing so you may end up sad, lonely and even hurt… why? The pussy or penis was only seasonal and by getting it back you created … NTP effect. What is the NTP effect? Glad you asked …. NTP effect means NOT THE PUSSY or NOT THE PENIS! You will never "love" that person the same. Now you have a whole new set of issues when the memory of the pussy or penis was fine the way it was… a memory. And a great memory if you asked me but who's asking who? Don't go after the old pussy or penis because it will never be the same again! You want the MTP effect and not the NTP effect.

Now, how many of you actually miss the pussy or penis and not the person? See, the truth doesn't hurt at all. Be real with yourself and you will be just fine. Now lay back and enjoy the ride …. think about all that good pussy or penis that has come into your life. And keep it as that … a memory! **#IMTP**

GET THE SHIRT

Melts In Your Mouth Not In Your Hand

Skin soft as silk and creamy as milk

Warm to the touch
Baby's breath, hush
COME WITH ME!
Your fingers run over my shoulder
Soft and gentle as a summer breeze
My breath is soft, and your fingers are warm
You move your fingers down my arms and to my hands
In and out you massage your hand within mine, we intertwine
So fine...
It feels warm and my breath is soft
You take your fingers around the back of my neck
I can feel your heartbeat; I can feel your breath
Your fingers are getting hot and my neck is getting wet
Hold my hair, so you can feel it!
My breaths get deep and I fan my face
Your fingers are working magic and my body needs grace
I bend my head down towards the floor
It's getting hot and my breath is getting deep
You move your fingers down my back
Around my shoulder blades in circles
The oil on your fingers are causing me to pulsate
My skin is soft, and your fingers are hot
Which makes for something in the melting pot?
If my skin feels like the baby bottom it is, combined with the heat of your
Love for me, that my friend is like melted chocolate...sweet!

Now back to me!
Open your eyes so you can see...
Your fingers are going down my back to the crack of my ass
It's a problem spot, relax!
Up and down, around and around, you're fingers, the oil, and the heat
You with me?
You take your fingers and bring them to the center of my back
You found my happy spot, now what?
You take your fingers as hot as they are and you slightly -
Like a Feathers butt brings them slow and mellow
My spot is like my favorite thing, to hit it right can make me sing
You brought it soft and you brought it hot... ooh my spot
You almost can't resist as your lips approach my tits
Stop
Breathing as hard as you are, your fingers are producing flames
Sweat is forming down my spine as you touch me again and again
You turn, and we see my nipples are against you
Your mouth opens with each deep breath you take
My body is weak and is filled with your heat
In your mouth does my tit find its way
The heat from your lips and the fire from your spit
Makes them hard and I can't take no more
I feel like I'm floating
The beauty of me... melts in your mouth and not in your hands!
Thanks for stopping by my friend!
Come again!

Summer and the Jets

It was a Saturday evening and I was getting ready to go out to a hotspot with some of my peoples. I love hanging out on a Saturday night, I wanna dance and just have fun…

I run my bath water; I love a hot bath, I add my oil and fresh scent, Chanel Gardenia is my favorite. I light my candles and turn down the lights. Time to be one with myself…

The water is steaming as I put the eye cloth over my eyes. The plasma is overhead and is playing soft music that is soothing to my soul.

I am totally in my element as I position my ass to sit in the mold that was created just for me… oh we, I just love being Summer B.

The music is taking me to another world. There will be no turning back. I hit the control for the jets to kick in as I hold on.

I hit the other control to turn the music slightly up so that I can continue to get my groove on. The JETS are doing its thing. The water is hot and there are beads of sweat…. on my lip.

The tub was design by Ms. B personally. One step up and you are in an oasis built for at least four, the deepness is like being in heaven, water over your shoulders and enough space to lay.

There are heated soap dispensers' and flowers all around. Marsha brings in fresh flowers every Friday morning so that Ms. B can enjoy them on her weekends. A Monet original sits over there so Ms. B can stare and enjoy the flair, while laying in her chase, made of silk and lace.

The plasma is 55 inches and encased in a beautiful frame. The windows are just gorgeous and a terrace that you can walk out. There is a small wine cooler and a bar with a towel warmer. When you step onto the floor, the heat begins to warm your toes.

You know what kind of kinky stuff can go on in Ms. B's bathroom. I mean imagine that you had all this, and your husband was worth every cent of it. You could be the shit... What? I'm just saying...

So, the jets are going, and the feel is soothing. Can you imagine anything better? I have all the time in the world today. No hotel, no hectic crazes... just Summer and the Jets.... The water is hot and there are beads of sweat... on my lip.

The phone rings and on the screen, the caller Id says it's Simply Sweet. I chuckle. Simply Sweet is the nickname I dubbed him.

It's what you say after you get a taste of him. Simply Sweet is what you feel after you un-curl your toes, kind of like milk chocolate soft and warm and just enough to tempt your tongue. I turn on the speaker phone and say hello to Simply Sweet as the jets are working their magic and the water is getting deep.

He is happy to talk to me, didn't know he could reach me. Usually he has to leave a couple of messages and wait for the reply. Did I say the water is hot and the steam is getting thick?

So how are you and what are you up to? In the tub relaxing my mind and my body is so ready to follow. I share with him what's been going on at the hotel lately, about the new business I'm starting, and he asked about my love life.

Did you hear a pen drop? I mean.... It's kind of dry.

He laughs and said, "You are a trip, always keeping people away". Well, what can I say? That's the best way so I can control my happy days. In the meantime, the water is hot, and the steam was thick about twenty minutes ago.

Lay your head back and close your eyes he says. The jets are in effect and Ms. B is laying back wondering what's in store. He softly says, "Imagine me there with you, in the tub right next to you".

As he says this my hand moves to my stomach and I rub my stomach with two fingers, round and round, this way and that way.

"I am massaging your shoulders as the water massages your skin.

Can you feel me deep within?" He says, "I nibble your ear and go down to your chest". My hand circles my nipples as I imagine his soft lips tasting my breast. What more can a girl ask for? I mean the girl lol.

My head is laid back and the jets are hella hot. The one that is directly in front of me was designed to keep the girl happy. When sitting in my personal spot the jet can reach the girl in no time at all. It's my favorite jet. What? I'm just saying...

Sweet says, "My mouth bites your shoulders very gently as you pant".

Hell, I can get down like that. My eyes are closed, and my mouth is wet, all this steam gone shrink a chic, but hell I'm down. What you gone do to me now?

"I bring you over to me where you sit on my lap and the jets tingle your Fannie as your arms and legs wraps all around me". My hand moves down to the girl and ....

The jets are getting heavier and my lip is covered in sweat. This whole story is getting soaking wet. S

So, he continues to tell me where he will put his lips on and the jet gets so heavy and my hand slips this way along with the story and the next thing I know, this fool is stepping into the window.

"Marsha saw the caller id in the kitchen, can see the light on the phone. When I rang the bell, she giggled. Knew you would get a kick out of seeing me... especially where you would be in the bath of ecstasy".

He removes his clothes as I jumped up with excitement. It's Simply Sweet when you call me, now make mommy holler!

He took her into his arms, she stripped him naked. They jumped into the tub with the jets directing their steps. She is digging this hotness.

He is rubbing her breast and her inner thighs …. nice.

She is rubbing his balls … sweet. He is feeling every moment of this love ecstasy.

His penis can't control himself. It's moving all alone. As she finds his nipples in her mouth and under her tongue.

Her girl is very wet and seems to be falling in love as we speak. The love drops, that are evading is pretty deeps.

He snatched her closer, injected his love …she pulsated his name, to Too Sweet, with love.

She walks in Beauty

Legs sway in with the beautiful creation. Somber smile as if to seduce you.

Shirt is penciled, and her shoes are Prada while her lips, she softly licks to the beating of her heart...

She walks in Beauty!

A deep breath as subtle as a baby, her chest rises as your head lifts in union.

The buttons on her shirt, three opens to her heart as you can hear it... hear her heart beat.

She walks in Beauty!

The smell of her being takes a hold and control of you as she possesses.

Your head turns, and your manhood is now controlling your emotions.

She walks in Beauty!

Her feet are tan, and her toes look as good as an ice pop on a hot summer day.

Her shoes say, "Come to me" and you begin to do just that...

She walked right pass me and hailed a cab, I'm left standing there with my mouth in my hand!

She walked in Beauty!

Now that, I understand!

My Heart Skips A Beat

As I sit here thinking of you, I can't help but to notice my heart skipping its beat
My vision of you as you walk into the room and the smile on your face you can't erase
As easy as it seems you hold me tight as I rub your jeans
And my back is against your chest and the way you grab my hair around and kiss

I can't help but to feel my heart beat harder and harder as the vision continues ….
Oh, my word, what's the name of that song?

You whisper in my ear as the heat comes from your lips
And the feeling that I get is like …. Imagine this:
It's cold outside, the fire is lit, you see me walk in with a gown of silk
My walk is this way and my walk goes that way as the gown front split open
Secures your view as instructed to ….
Your lip starts to drop as I call out your name … amazing grace.
You are sweating out beads as fast as an oozy and your pants are swelling fast as I arrive at my destination, a sweet sensation as good as this will always leave you, rousingly speechless.
My poetry is getting me wet …. Summer B the poetic mistress

Summer's Rain

The rain drops fall on the glass roof of the flower room
She can feel his heartbeat...
She takes a deep breath, rubs her forehead with her backhand
Chest rise, breath heavy, thoughts many
The smell of rain on a quite so sunny day can be breathtaking
The flowers are wet yet dry all at the same time
Her boots match her shorts and her hair is swaying with her smile
Cute...
The rain continues as she plays in the flower beds
Thinking of him... the man
The rain always makes her think of him
He's Summer's rain...
She smiles, finds the perfect rose, deep red
She can feel his heart beat harder
She takes the rose and clips the thorns
Thump thump it continues...
She smells the rose and can feel him holding her
As she closes her eyes, she can feel his heartbeat
The beat is getting harder
She steps out into the rain... the garden is beautiful in the fall
Variations of color at best and the tree...
The tree is where she and the man first became friends
She walks into the rain and her hair is starting to drip
She hurries her step...its wet
She stands under the tree with a smile on her face as she thinks of
him
The rain continues, and she must go in
She can feel his arms wrapped tightly around her as if to not let go

SUMMER BRADSHAU

She grabs herself as she makes her way to the cottage leaving the tree to be

Her shirt is wet, and her hair is dripping as she opens the door to the sun room

She hears the recorder... "Thinking of you" and the dial tone

She stops, and she stares at the recorder over there and the look on her face

Her heart enters a race and her voice tries to say...

She shakes her head and the water makes a sprinkling show

Take off her boots, puts on her shoes, wipes her face and continues

Place the rose into a glass on the table with a smile

Summer's rain on a quite so sunny day.

Johnny Blaze...

Summer B just left the hotel and is off to the cottage sitting off the water down a country road. You can hear the roosters in the background and birds singing happiness by the window. It's 5:30 am and she just got a call from a friend... says he is on the way in. The hot chocolate is hot, and the whip cream is thick.

Down the windy road and into the gate, I can hear his motorcycle engine... oh wee! I run out to the porch as I see him ride in, two jimmies to the wind. My skirt is blowing, and my hair is whisking this way and that way. My bare feet are slightly cold but that's ok. The anticipation of Johnny Blaze can get me that way. I live for those phone calls at 3 freaking am. Usually I am able to roll over with a smile, he will be here in a while, but the hotel had an event, fundraising to help the homeless.

The fire from the back of the bike leaves a trail and leaves it hot. That man right there knows just what to do when Summer b is feeling blue. Her Facebook status was this: Only the lonely can live this life call   777-9311...now that's the Times song if you remember, that's nice.

When Johnnie's girl saw Summer's profile she immediately woke Johnny up and said your girl is in trouble.

He checked her status and scrolled down the page... damn, we can't have Summer in distress it's too close to the date.

Johnnie's girl knows the routine... it was 1:17 in the morning. Summer was online, and her ego was in trouble. Says she has not been able to produce a lick, haven't even been able to secure...

Well, I packed a bag and kissed my chic. She knows who is number one, my reality depends on it. Give her the credit card so she can shop compliments of me and I am off in the wind to see my Summer B... sweet.

When Johnny Blaze comes to town Summer comes alive. He sparks her fire. Helmet off and his gear, four hours of riding and the wind just set in, I want some hot chocolate but maybe some Gin.

That ride is something else but well worth my time, my damsel in distress, pouty smile, super-hot. Kiss those soft lips and down to her neck, tap that ass with my hand and good morning princess.

Johnny is smiling at me... sweet!

He doesn't want to hear my pain he only wants to see my smile. It's been a while. I have been able to secure Happiness, I even sell it in a bottle, Fountain of Youth and "The Girl" Barbie doll, comes with a scent too. Lol it's cute... but my reality is, I have an issue.

My assistant has made us breakfast and it smells good too, pancakes and bacon with strawberries and whip cream. I like whip cream, it's cold and thick.

He joins me next to the fire. It's dark outside and it is slightly chilly, got the mink rug open and I'm feeling giddy. All work and no play make for a dull Summer B... can we get her going again. I don't like it when she is all work and no play, she might cut somebody by the end of the day.

Back to the fire and the breakfast at hand...
He has a bag in his backpack and it is just for me... oh wee summer b. got some new panties.

Johnny is smart and not like the rest, you see he has a drawer full of this shit and everyone know not to even think about it. "That drawer there is for Summer you see. If you try to wear any of those undies you are going to have to deal with me"! He travels the world and as his venture is free he picks up all sorts of cute undies, just for me... Summer B (can you see me smiling?)

So, I excitedly look in the bag, I already know I will like them, silky smooth, very sheer, they are blue with a red heart in between. Never have I seen such as this, these are simply sweet!

They even have a cute little smell, how well do you remember me, it's Chanel. I am happy already and we only just begun. How long are you staying Johnny, how much time do I get?

While we are eating our breakfast and mimosas to tilt, he is smiling at me. I pretend not to see...
Down by the fire with a glass in my hand, I am full of happiness and the bacon helped. Bacon is my favorite lol.

Johnny comes and sits with me, brushes my hair back and kisses my forehead, his little girl again. Ok, back to reality. I like it when he smiles at me. Makes me feel complete, it's not easy being Summer B.

I lay on his lap and he rub his fingers through my hair, his face I do stare. What kind of man drops all on his plate, drives four hours in the wind to make sure I'm straight, something a girl can appreciate.

The mimosa and strawberries Gina gave us is cute, she knows what I like and so does Johnny Blaze, he gone make me live again. The energy from him can last a while if he can make me smile, I'm smiling cause I'm a flower and he's the water, watch me grow.

He turns me over and kisses my back, takes his finger, just one finger and rubs down to my crack. He knows just how this makes me feel, I get a chill and the feeling is real. It's the best feeling that a girl could ever get, one finger, nice and slow makes a girl wanna …. When did you say you were leaving?

I love when he uses the finger; my back has been up in a whack, working late and early too, no fun in the bag, no new Jimmie Choo's. I have not even been shopping in over three months now you know I'm gone cut somebody if I don't get some new clothes. Back to the back at hand...my friend.

He massages the rest and he knows how I like it, deep over here yet soft as a baby's blanket. I have one of those, so I can feel loved, I got the blue one out and it smells like a dove. I like my baby's blanket; it's so soft and sweet. Makes me wanna do me, oooh wee Summer B.

After the back, he heads for the thighs, soft as silk, hot as fire he is in for the attack, the girl has awoken and is ready for some attention. It has been one of those weeks, hormones doing fireworks all over the city. Almost snatched up the mailman, lol.... But really! It's been a minute.

He gets up and grabs my hand, takes me to another land, the hammock out back under the tree oooh wee, Johnny Blaze, what you gone do to me... He grabs my hair and brushes it backs. He leans in and kisses my lips ... lay your head back, it was like this (leaning in kissing you)

His tongue was slowly moving down my throat and back to my lips he did kiss. Amazing how much good you can feel when the right person is part of the deal.

He is moving his hands to my ass. I feel the heat from his lips as he kisses my neck and hands I feel him squeeze. This is sweet, as I bite my lip. He sucks my neck harder as I take his shoulders in my hands and after he bites into me, I scream a scream of ecstasy.

He takes his pelvis and intertwine with mine. The heat, the wetness, the ... taste of this.

Summer B and her energy is coming back to reality. The love she feels ... the orgasm he brings.

I see almonds in the sky, sun is beaming, water flow streaming right by while my guy is rubbing my feet to the sound of the birds going... chirp, chirp, it's tickling.
Johnny Blaze and Summer B...

(as I am writing this story... I am wearing the underwear that Johnny has given me. Black, lace and seductive. Gives me the inspiration to write in detail. And because I chose his underwear to write in, he also is my lead character in this story. I love wearing my cute little gifts. Your undies can end up in a story as this, but first you have to go shopping and send them in: Virtual message me.... I'm googable, google me oooh that tickles.

Come Take A Bath With Me

The bath water is running as I sit here brushing my hair, the steam is rising and so am I

my thoughts they go to you ...
My eyes are remembering the soft touch, your warm embrace, the look on your face
memories cannot erase
The fire is blazing as the steam is rising, the hotter the water gets the hotter I get
I cannot deny the thoughts you give me
Like running naked in a field of daisies, on a bright and sunny day
the memory will forever stay
I finish brushing and I get in, the water is now up to my chin
my vision of us is wrapped in a view
My fingers make traces, I use one and then two, around my breast, around my nipple
down to my belly around they go
Where will they stop, no one will know
the water is wet, and the steam is hot
I can feel my heart stop...
now close your eyes and dream of me
I'm your poetic mistress ... Ms. summer b

Amazing Grace, How Sweet The Sound

She stepped into the room and your heart ... it skipped a beat
She seemed to have tranquilized the room with her presence
Everyone has fixed their mouth and caught the drool that escaped
from the lips
Her smile is contagious, and her step is high and light
She seems to glow with every flow of potion penetrating your nose
Your eyes are wide open
Her laughter makes you perspire and you can't stop glaring her way
She smells of beautiful butterfly and heavenly bliss
Wrapped, around your fingertips
She stepped into the room and your heart . . . It skipped a beat

Wrapped Up

Wrapped in heat from the love that is pouring out within
    STOP... bring it back
Watching with temptation and visions not pure
Craving the sweetness of the skin
    STOP... now forward
Making the sweat roll off your head and onto...
Feeling as if hunting for red October in the midst
     STOP... right there
Allowing pleasures of the unknown
Penetrate your soul
     STOP ...now explode!
I see you man'd up, and came again my friend

My Poetry is Motionless...

I find it hard to believe the words that I hear. They flow from one's mouth without warning. Sometimes it rhymes, and I laugh to myself. Sometimes it gets deep with feelings. I put it on paper and it all seems to fade as I write with a flow from within. A blank stare I may carry, and my brow is a frown as I try to determine my pace. My pen does not write as I get into grove and I write only words that are blank. My poetry is motionless...

Can you hear what I'm saying as I say it within? No words are making much sense. I can pretend to please you with big fancy words, they can rhyme and jive you to tears. But what I want to feel is so real. It must make and take you by surprise and let you know what you hear are more than just words, but my pen does not move as I get into the grove and I write only words that are blank... my poetry is motionless.

FRIDAY NIGHT WITH SUMMER B...

OOH WEE!

It's Friday night and you are feeling a little frisky. You decide to go out with some friends at work. It's happy hour time and your skirt is cute. Your shirt dips low and your lip gloss is fresh... girl you a hot mistress.

We arrive at our favorite hot spot. It's jumping when we walk in. The DJ is playing the "meet me at the dance floor"

I'm at the bar of my favorite hot spot, sipping on a green apple martini, it's the drink for me. I am tapping my feet to the beat of the music. I love the music; I come for the dance...

So, I'm enjoying myself when in walks Mr. Wonderful. He stands about 6'1, tan skin, boat slacks and loafers. His shoulders are large, and his build is sweet, he is like, ooh wee! He is the shit. Look straight at the front of his pants to catch a glimpse of his stiff. I mean, he walked in here like the stallion that he is and suddenly, I stare at his face... I am like, Chris? I used to do his ass.

This dude was the bomb, had it all and I passed it by. You know how that go...

So, he stopped, and he looked, and he picked me up off the floor. My skirt came up as he twirled me around and dropped me back down... again. Boy my head start to spin.

He smells good as I the same. Two different worlds coming together again. When I last saw him, he was begging me to stay, but I had to leave, he was falling in love with me. Love is just a four-letter word. Shhh, can you hear it? No, yeah so that's what I say about love.

Anyway, he smells so good, takes me back to the crib with the 1 a.m. glass of gin. Make me wanna call his name, damn, he ain't changed. So, I am smiling and laughing and touching his arm. He is smiling and laughing and sizing me up. Says I lost weight and I look great and wow, you are still the bomb. I'm laughing all the way to the bank, you think I ain't...

And I'm like yeah what you think that you were the only one who can do me? I don't crumble without someone in my life. I continue to flourish and ....

WHAT THE HELL! This fool done grabbed me and started kissing me. His tongue is in my mouth and his breath is so fresh and hot. People are looking they are starting to stop. He has me leaned back and my legs are slightly bent. My arm is dangling down there, and the girl just caught a whiff...

Oh boy, you done woke up the lady. I don't know about you but I'm about to fall on the floor. Wtf

Does this man ever leave anything out or does he just go straight for the orgasm right there on the spot. Everyone is staring and laughing and then when he lifts me up and stands me back tall, he straightens my shoulders and wipes my lips, the room, they clap and cheer and hiss... this is some shit. Ooh wee...

He looks at me and he can't believe what he sees. It's me... Summer b

He grabs me by the hand and asks if I was with friends... no and out the door we go. So...

Where do we go? I don't know (laughing out loud)

Says he's in town for a conference, check this out, this brother works for Trojans... He got condoms! galore... oh, back to the door. We go to his room at the Bradshau Hotel; Penthouse Suite is how he do. And ... You?

So, he calls room service and he's whispering in the phone, takes his time, smiles at me and pretends he's not mesmerized. I used to make him call my name back in the day... Summer B... oh excuse me... back to the story.

So, room service arrives and it's beautiful at best. Grapes that he can feed me as I lay across his chest. There is cheese and light crisp, strawberries with a chocolate kiss. There are green apples sliced up over there, dipped in caramel nice and hot, ooh wee, I love being Summer b.

Sit on the couch and turn the music on, a song that I recall. I jump up and I dance, dance on over to where he stands. He's a handsome man my friends. I mean the man is bad. Ooh wee...

He lays me back on his lap. He rubs my head very softly as if holding a feather. Breathing softly as our breaths form a union. Together we look into each other's eyes. And at that very moment the girl spoke up and said, "why do it take you three years to do what you got to do"? She startled me, and I giggled.

He reaches over and takes a stem of grapes. Plucks them off and feeds them to me as I lay on his lap.   After feeding me the grapes, he sings a little to me and he rubs his fingers on my neck. Soft and gentle like cotton on a baby's hands. It tingled, and I giggled...

He takes the top button and unbuttoned it slowly, staring into my eyes. My eyes are focused on him at all times. My chest, it starts to rise. My breaths are deep and It's getting hot inside. ...

He moves on to the next button and the girl is laughing out loud. I am like, goodness you are too ghetto. Can't take you anywhere...

He is on the third and he has two to go, I can feel the heat flow. He opens my shirt and plays with my bra. Black lace is what I was wearing and black satin bows. I am cute, and it is hot! Am I going through menopause or something?

He takes his fingertips and runs them around my nipples, it tickles, and I giggle...

CLOSE YOUR EYES so you can see, the VISION of ME... ooh pretty!

So, the girl is laughing loud, she thinks it's all good. So, my guy is working his fingers around my naval, and he is able cause I'm digging this. He rubs my cheeks and plays with my nose, its cold. He runs his fingers through my hair, like he cares. I stare...

My buttons are making their way undone... I can hear your heartbeat. I can... hear it beat. Sweet!

I love the way he caresses me. Gentle as a Summer Breeze, he is a tease, geese. But I'm in because I just love this man. He takes off his shirt and I take off mine. I take his shirt out of his hand and smell's it, it smells like him. I put it on and I smile at him, boy look at that grin. He gone get that girl started...

I hold the shirt in my hand as I smell my shoulder, it smells like him. Now look at MY grin. I look up at him and he puts his hand on my forehead. Like a feather, in his hand, he is the man... no really, he is "the man".

I am hot like fire and my thighs are heavy, the girl is awake, and she wants BIG DADDY. What is a girl to do? I mean. I am hot, and my thighs are heavy, I weigh a buck and a quarter and it aint even May yet. I'm drowning, in downy.

I feel my toes tingle and I giggle... how sweet! Ooh wee...

He pulls my jeans down past my knees, NOW BREATHE... good grief. Pay attention please. Now, where was I?

Ok... he pulls my jeans down past my knees, he wants to rub my legs and he can. Off comes the jeans and at the same time the girl is making a command that I get on with the plan and out comes my hand and where it lands... made new friends and this man in my hand came again! and again! And again!

My girl got tingled and I giggled while we ran into the hot tub... Who can find the rubber ducky?

92 pairs of Underwear

Back when I first started losing weight I went out shopping for a pair of cute underwear because I was writing and needed a quick lift me up in life to get me going. When one of my clients saw my cute underwear, she encouraged me to buy more...

After I purchased more, my clients started buying me fancy cute underwear as an effort to Upgrade ourselves and to motivate me to keep writing my stories.

I have some really cute underwear. Some have rhinestone and other initials.

I have lace and satin, spandex (not recommended for venting issues, never wear them) and cotton. But they are all so cute and colorful and happy and sexy too. Oh... and sexy too! (Did I say that already?)

I get underwear from admirers and clients and sometimes companies send me underwear, so I advertise for them. My clients always buy when they send something cute, so it's a win win for everyone.

So, my 92 pairs of underwear and counting. It's spring time so it's time to get shopping!

I'm Summer B and I just love being ME!

NOTE: IN SUMMER'S STORIES...SUMMER B is wearing what type of panties? Summer has a thing for underwear, she likes them cute and sexy with lots of thrills. What kind should she wear in her next short story? You choose! Send her a pair (small and mediums) by September 15th, 2018 and she will choose the best of the best in her next story which will end up in the next erotic book, which can lead to a mention of your name, maybe. (laughing)

Your Favorite Titles and your Favorite Quote on a T-shirt, mug etc.

Visit our virtual site for more information about how to secure yours while they are in stock.

Thank You for taking a shower with me ...

This book as well as Purgatory Living, and a few more books to come is created to help grow our Homeless to Humanity Project.

Homeless to Humanity and our Transitions of Life projects are to help teach cities how to solve homelessness and to help individuals and families rebirth themselves back into humanity from poverty etc. Together with Hand & Hand Foundation we will work hard to create a program that is beneficial to the communities of people.

Helping to secure housing, pay deposits, rents etc. as part of the project as well as basic life skills to help ensure future knowledge of life security.

We will help provide training for jobs, nutrition, health and living as the project grows. We will secure through purchase and donations, housing and resources for individuals and families that qualify under the proper guidelines.

Be a part of the solution by purchasing our books and or donating to the project. Have a book signing and invite your colleagues, family and friends to help support the project. With your donations and book purchases, you can help a family get off the streets and into some warm sheets.

#ThinkAboutIt We spend money on useless things in life, we waste money each and every day, so why not help those in need by purchasing some good books or donating to a great cause that will help save a huge population of our good people.

It's not always the fault of an individual as to how life pans out. Someone must give you a job or someone must give you the money to live your life. Life unfortunately is not free and there will always be individuals who will need a helping hand. If it's not you, it's someone else regardless of race, religion or breed.

EROTIC SHOWERS

Help us help humanity by being leaders in our communities of people. Our actions and our words will help or break people along the way. Be of love, be of action, be of positive forces of energy!

BE THE CHANGE THE WORLD NEEDS and join me, in saving humanity! One book at a time and one life at a time. Together, lives can be saved!

www.facebook.com/groups/eroticshower

Email: Insummersworld@gmail.com